DECORATE LIFE :

SCRAPBOOK

BACKGROUNDS   8

BORDERS   20

MATTES   36

TITLES & WORDAGE   52

EMBELLISHMENTS   66

JOURNALING   86

MIX IT UP   100

BOOK END   114

CONTENTS

Create layouts that are every bit as fresh and smart as they are simple to duplicate and adapt. Now, start Decorating Life.

DECORATE LIFE : SCRAPBOOK

TITLES TRANSFORM

MAKE MONOGRAMS

GREAT DIVIDES

PHOTO MONTAGES

FABRIC FOUNDATIONS

MIX AND MATCH

SEW SIMPLE

STITCH PATTERNS

ARRANGE STICKERS

CREATE COLLAGES

1
BACKGROUNDS

TITLES TRANSFORM

TYPOGRAPHY AS A BACKGROUND

EIGHTIES CHILD BY LONI STEVENS

[THE 1980'S.] A DECADE OF CRIMPED HAIR; BANANA CLIPS; JELLY SHOES; DEBBIE GIBSON; DURAN-DURAN; ET; CYNDI LAUPER; THE KARATE KID; STRAWBERRY SHORTCAKE DOLLS; ATARI; STONEWASHED JEANS; FLUORESCENT NEON CLOTHES; ONE-PIECE LEOTARDS; BREAK DANCING; THE FAMILY STATION-WAGON; JAWS; PLASTIC STREAMERS ON THE HANDLE BARS OF YOUR BIKE; PONY TAIL TO THE SIDE OF YOUR HEAD; CLIPS THAT WOULD HOLD YOUR SHIRT IN A KNOT ON THE SIDE; YOU WORE SOCKS OVER TIGHTS, WITH HIGH-TOP REEBOKS; YOU WORE LIKE 8 PAIRS OF SOCKS AT ONCE, SCRUNCHED DOWN; NEW KIDS ON THE BLOCK; PAC MAN; LEG WARMERS; ROTARY DIAL TELEPHONES; STAR SEARCH; L.A. GEAR; MIAMI VICE; DUKES OF HAZZARD; FOOTLOOSE; TAPE CASSETTES; BOOM BOXES; PERMED HAIR; STAR WARS; YOU PEGGED THE BOTTOM OF YOUR JEANS; POUND PUPPIES; CAREBEARS. [MY CHILDHOOD.]

reflect

(TIP)
CREATE A PATTERN WITH CAPTIVATING TYPOGRAPHY

TITLES TRANSFORM

MAKE MONOGRAMS

GREAT DIVIDES

PHOTO MONTAGES

FABRIC FOUNDATIONS

MIX AND MATCH

SEW SIMPLE

STITCH PATTERNS

ARRANGE STICKERS

CREATE COLLAGES

1
BACKGROUNDS

TITLES TRANSFORM

[THE 1980's.] A DECADE OF CRIMPED HAIR; BANANA CLIPS; JELLY SHOES; DEBBIE GIBSON; DURAN-DURAN; ET; CYNDI LAUPER; THE KARATE KID; STRAWBERRY SHORTCAKE DOLLS; ATARI; STONEWASHED JEANS; FLUORESCENT NEON CLOTHES; ONE-PIECE LEOTARDS; BREAK DANCING; THE FAMILY STATION-WAGON; JAWS; PLASTIC STREAMERS ON THE HANDLE BARS OF YOUR BIKE; PONY TAIL TO THE SIDE OF YOUR HEAD; CLIPS THAT WOULD HOLD YOUR SHIRT IN A KNOT ON THE SIDE; YOU WORE SOCKS OVER TIGHTS, WITH HIGH-TOP REEBOKS; YOU WORE LIKE 8 PAIRS OF SOCKS AT ONCE, SCRUNCHED DOWN; NEW KIDS ON THE BLOCK; PAC MAN; LEG WARMERS; ROTARY DIAL TELEPHONES; STAR SEARCH; L.A. GEAR; MIAMI VICE; DUKES OF HAZZARD; FOOTLOOSE; TAPE CASSETTES; BOOM BOXES; PERMED HAIR; STAR WARS; YOU PEGGED THE BOTTOM OF YOUR JEANS; POUND PUPPIES; CAREBEARS. [MY CHILDHOOD.]

reflect

(TIP)

CREATE A PATTERN WITH CAPTIVATING TYPOGRAPHY

MAKE MONOGRAMS

EXPLORE

(THE JOY OF DISCOVERY)

Matthew's end-of-school program for kindergarten was held outside at the Jr. High, right next door to his school. Jodi & Nathan were up from Las Vegas looking for land to build on so we took three-year old Mikayla with us to his program. It ended up being a rather lengthy program, as we watched each grade, from kindergarten to sixth, perform their musical skits. And it was hot! Mikayla started to complain so after Matthew's class performed Mikayla and I broke away from the program and walked across the field to the drinking fountain. On the way back Mikayla couldn't help but pick every dandelion she spotted on the field! It was fun to watch her excitement as she closed her eyes and blew the feathery petals off the stem and then would open them last minute to watch them float away. And what a great distraction from the heat! I love this age when they still get excited over the smallest of discoveries!

THE JOY OF DISCOVERY

(TIP)

USE THE SHAPE AND PATTERN OF LETTER STICKERS

GREAT DIVIDES

RIBBONS AND TRIM

EMILY BY MARIA GRACE ABUZMAN

(TIP)

UNITE COLOR BLOCKS BY COVERING SEAMS

THINGS

I LOVE

my room

Pineapple
DE 144

Danish Moss
DE 241

Ruffles
DE 660
(A)

I love

LINCOLN LOGS
THE ORIGINAL

toys & games

stuffed

animals

BASKET
BEANIES
ty

my family

riding my bike

helping

swimming

Painting

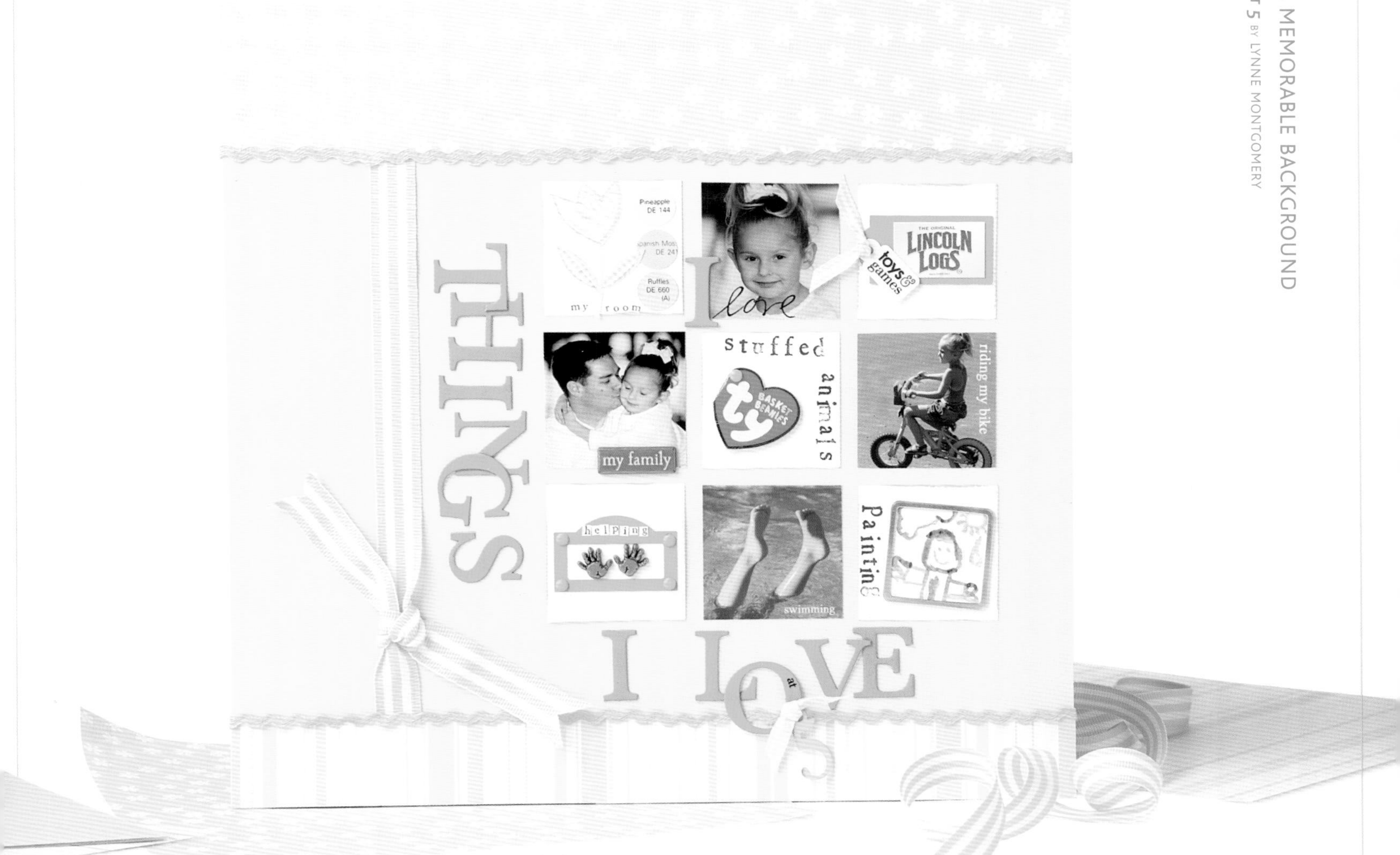

(TIP)
ANCHOR DESIGN VISUALLY BY USING
RIBBON AS A VERTICAL BORDER

what a *Flirt*

What's better than an armful of flowers from my sweet boys? You and Daddy surprised me with this pretty bouquet on May Day. Instead of handing the flowers to me, though, you dropped them at my feet! Your delivery method may need a little work!

may DAY

(TIP)

FRAY, FOLD OR LAYER THIS
VERSATILE MEDIUM

SUMMER 2005

Finding LILY

Chris and I were so excited to give Daisy her new puppy! We had it all planned out...Chris had promised Daisy before she left for the coast that he was going to have a surprise on her bed when she got home. So he put a toy veterinarian kit on her bed with a stuffed puppy inside, and we hid the real puppy in a box in her closet. We were all ready at 6 for her to get home, but she never showed up. I finally called Rigdon, only to find out that he hadn't even left the coast yet and wasn't going to be home until 10! We were so upset that our plans were ruined. When she finally got home, we went through the whole routine again, hoping the puppy would be quiet until Daisy discovered her. Daisy walked in and discovered the stuffed puppy on her bed, then looked just a wee bit sad about it. However, when she opened the door to her closet and her little pup was looking at her, she couldn't stop grinning! It was worth every bit of trouble we went to over the weekend to get that puppy to her and see the priceless look on her face!

DARLING

PUPPY

(TIP)
LAYERING PAPER OR FABRIC IN THE SAME
COLOR FAMILY UNITE THE PAGE OR CARD

BEAUTIFUL *bride*

Our niece, Missy, on her wedding day. We have never seen her look as lovely as she did that day. She was the perfect picture of grace and beauty. It made us so happy to see her in love.

Melissa Jobson Laws
Saturday, June 18, 2005

(TIP) FOR A SUBTLE SOPHISTICATED LOOK, USE THREAD THAT MATCHES THE BACKGROUND OR LEAVE OUT THE THREAD AND ENJOY THE HOLE PATTERNS

STITCH PATTERNS

Married

Missy and Bret had a gorgeous outdoor wedding. They both looked so beautiful as they said their vows beneath a trellis of ivy and flowers.

Mr. and Mrs. Bret Laws
Saturday, June 18, 2005

(TIP)
USE COMPLIMENTARY COLOR FOR
A CONTRASTING BACKGROUND

ARRANGE STICKERS

FORM A PATCHWORK PATTERN

CAMRYN BY KRIS STANGER

(TIP)

DISTRESS OR PAINT EDGES OF STICKERS FOR A VINTAGE LOOK

CREATE COLLAGES

COMBINE STRIPS OF PATTERNED AND PLAIN PAPER

HER PINK SHOES BY JENNIFER JENSEN

(TIP) LEAVE A SMALL SPACE BETWEEN EACH STRIP
TO REVEAL CONTRASTING PAPER UNDERNEATH

STACK STICKERS

LAYER

NOTIONS

COMBINE TRIMS

FINISHED BUTTONS

BORDERS BLOOM

FILE FOLDER TABS

PAINT AND DISTRESS

PHOTOS AS BORDERS

PUNCHING HOLES

LABEL THIS

CONNECTED

RIBBONS ON SEAMS

BRAIDING FLOSS

2
BORDERS

STACK STICKERS

(TIP)
RIBBONS AND PAPER OF THE SAME COLOR
VALUE WILL COMPLIMENT EACH OTHER

LAYER

RIBBON AND STICKERS

AN ELEMENT OF CHILDHOOD BY JENNIFER JENSEN

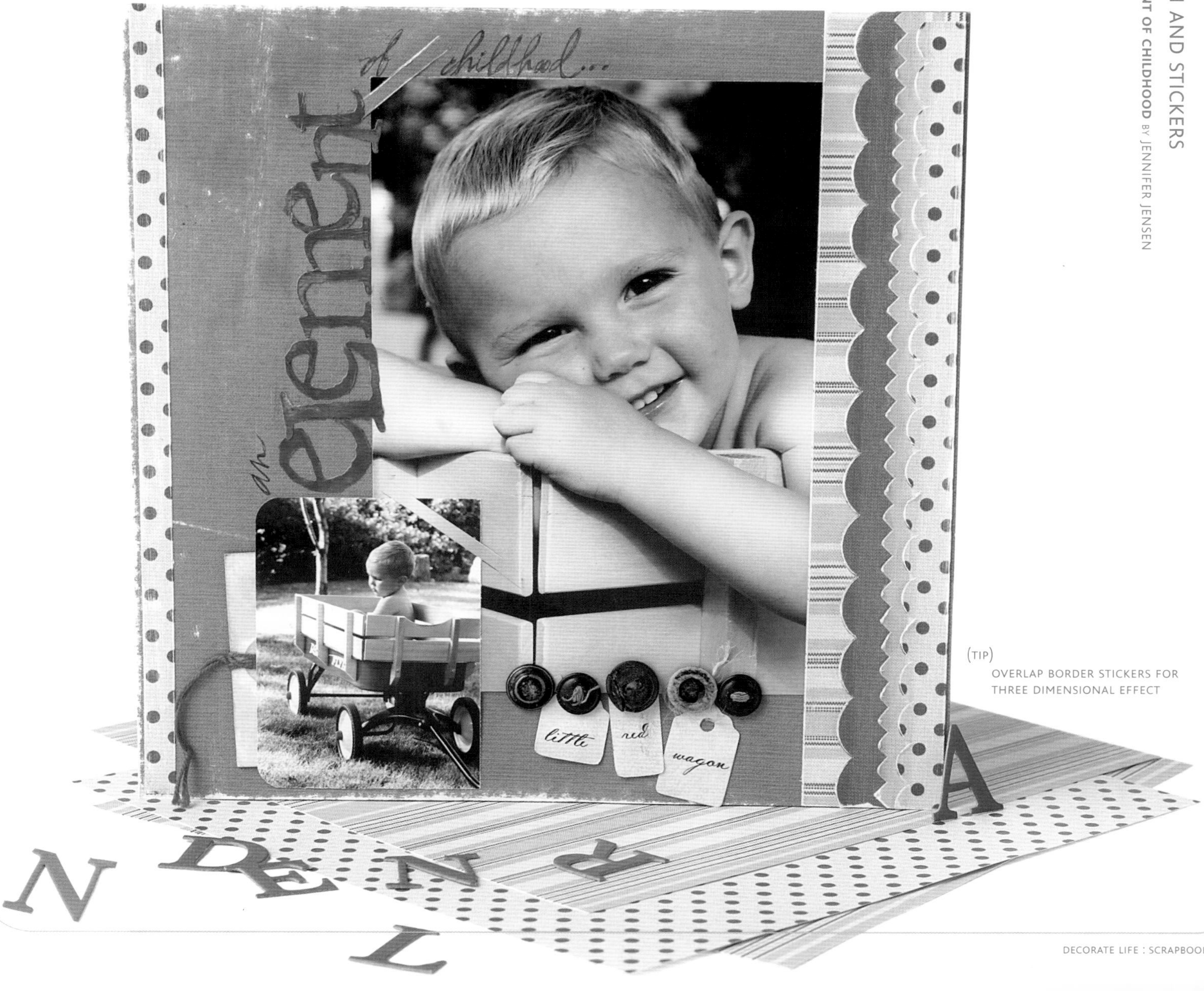

an element of childhood...
little
red
wagon

(TIP)

OVERLAP BORDER STICKERS FOR THREE DIMENSIONAL EFFECT

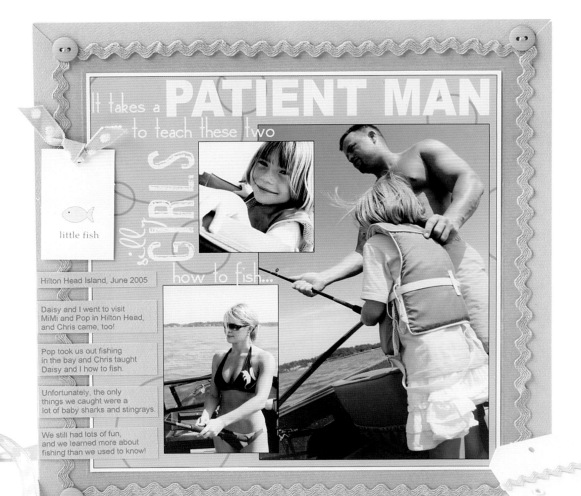

It takes a **PATIENT MAN** to teach these two *silly* **GIRLS** how to fish...

little fish

Hilton Head Island, June 2005

Daisy and I went to visit
MiMi and Pop in Hilton Head,
and Chris came, too!

Pop took us out fishing
in the bay and Chris taught
Daisy and I how to fish.

Unfortunately, the only
things we caught were a
lot of baby sharks and stingrays.

We still had lots of fun,
and we learned more about
fishing than we used to know!

(TIP)
RIC RAC AND BUTTONS MAKE THE ORDINARY EXTRAORDINARY

CHiCKS

grace was so **excited** when grandma gave her baby chicks for **EASTER** !!! i think that the poor little guys were trained well from the beginning... because she **CUDDLED** them and carried them everywhere she went ! i never knew that **CHICKENS** could make such great **PETS** for little girls, but grace has opened my eyes to a lot of new things !

(TIP)
LAYER VARIOUS TEXTURES, SIZES AND COLORS FOR A FRESH EFFECT

FINISHED BUTTONS

Our beautiful girl is so full of life – it makes us smile just to look at her!

Kaitlyn

3/04

(TIP) USE THREAD, FIBER OR RIBBONS EITHER TIED OR SEWN THROUGH THE HOLES

ADD DIMENSION WITH SINGLE
OR MULTIPLE FLOWERS
TOOTHLESS-YOU BY JOY BOHON

TOOTHLESS

YOU

On this day you were a very proud little girl. You see, you aren't so good at being the last to do anything, or to get anything , and well, you really were the last amongst your friends to get a loose tooth. That was quite a hard one for you. But finally, at age six, miracle of all miracles, it happened to you. You wiggled that tooth, you talked about it, you showed everyone with pride... and one day you were brave enough to let me push on it just a bit harder.. and the tooth was finally gone. There was that look on your face-of pride, of bewilderment, of excitement- all intermingled. Then came the tooth fairy, the stories and of course the photographs. This was my very favorite photo of them all. Congrats to you girl on a natural milestone. It makes me smile to see the delight in your eyes. June 2005

(TIP)
FINISH OFF FLOWERS WITH
VINTAGE BRADS FOR CONTRAST

FILE FOLDER TABS

TALENTED '53 BY LYNNE MONTGOMERY

TaLentEd '53

My mother is quite a talented lady. Although it all started years ago with dancing, modeling, and playing musical instruments her talents have evolved over the years to include sewing, needlepoint, oil painting, tole painting, jewelry making, gourmet cooking, furniture refinishing, wallpapering, decorating, and most recently paper arts. This is in addition to being a mother, mentor, teacher and highly respected school administrator.

ModEl

DanCer

MuSiciAn

Her example has rubbed off on me motivating me to develop my own talents and reminding me it's never too late to learn new things.

(TIP)
BEAUTIFUL PAPERS CAN TURN A COMMON FILE FOLDER INTO AN EXQUISITE BORDER TREATMENT

PAINT AND DISTRESS

(TIP)
BOLD AND VERSATILE CHIPBOARD TAKES ON JUST
THE RIGHT SHAPE AND COLOR FOR YOUR PAGE

(TIP)

SUPPORT THE MAIN SHOT WITH A VARIETY OF SMALLER PHOTOGRAPHS

Karli and Tyler have always had this special bond that is hard to even describe. She is such a sweetheart to him – always including him, helping him and looking after him. It started before Tyler was even talking and their friendship has continued to grow ever since. In fact, Tyler often tells me that Karli is his favorite friend! I have worried about Tyler having friends because of his autism... thank goodness for people like Karli who don't care whether or not he fits the mold of a "typical" child. She loves him for who he is and she somehow sees beyond the surface – looks deeper and connects with his heart and soul... thanks Karli.

(TIP)
CIRCLE PUNCHES EMPHASIZE THE CURVE OF THE DESIGN AND ALLOW
A VIEW OF THE BACKGROUND THROUGH NEGATIVE SHAPES

(TIP)
STRING SOME THOUGHTS TOGETHER
WITH RIBBON AND BLOSSOMS

LABEL HOLDERS CREATE
A NON-TRADITIONAL BORDER
LOVE ENDURES BY MELLETTE BEREZOSKI

endures

Starting a new life in a different country. Everything you owned in one suitcase. Raising three young children without any support. Overcoming hurdles and hardships with dignity and grace. Struggling. Being there for each other. Holding on and moving on. Surviving. Loving without conditions. Enduring. *Because that's what love is.*

Mom and Dad. Still in love after 40 years together. 2005

(TIP)
MAKE THE CONNECTION WITH RIBBON,
STICKERS, PAPER AND PHOTOS

RIBBONS ON SEAMS

Classic
cutie

baby k
6 months

(TIP)
SHEER RIBBON AND PASTEL BLOSSOMS ARE A CLASSIC COMBINATION

somethin special
not just your ordinary girl

Of course, every mother feels their child is something special. I admit that I'm the first to regularly boast about silly ordinary things such as how you put your own shoes on the right feet today without any help. I'll always be your biggest fan because I love you and it's impossible for me to be impartial. However, there is one thing that makes me gleam with pride which is completely unique and warranted for bragging, and that is your brilliant creativity. You are the queen of make believe, and beyond that of a typical three year old. You amaze me when I sit back and watch you play, draw, or act out a story using your fingers as characters. Your ability for abstract thought and comprehension is undoubtedly genious. You may encounter people throughout your life who will happen to miss this extraordinary trait, but never second guess yourself. You truly are something special beyond ordinary measure. Combined with your tender-hearted compassion, I can't wait to see the difference you're going to make in this world and the lives of the people around you. Mine, for one, will never be the same just because you're in it, you beautiful, amazing, three year old sweetheart.

(TIP)
COLORS COMBINE BEAUTIFULLY WHEN WOVEN TOGETHER

3
MATTES

FRAMED TAGS

TAG IT

INSTANT VINTAGE

METAL MATTES

FABRIC FRAMES

BEAUTIFUL BLOSSOMS

RUB-ONS

PERFECT PAPER

PAINT METAL

INTERLACE RIBBONS

METAL MESH

GLITTER MATTES

CHIPBOARD LETTERS

VELLUM LAYERS

(TIP)
CUT PAPER IN A TAG SHAPE TO MAKE A CARD BASE, THEN ADD A VINTAGE FRAME

TAG IT

MAKE A DISTINCTIVE BACKDROP

GREAT MARRIAGE BY LYNNE MONTGOMERY

A great marriage is not when the "perfect couple" come together. It's when an imperfect couple learns to enjoy their differences.

(TIP)
MOUNT PHOTOS ON TAGS FOR ADDED TEXTURE

INSTANT VINTAGE

(TIP)
USE PAINT AND FOAM STAMPS TO
CREATE A MATTE DIRECTLY ON PHOTO

I lo... ...you look... Sum... You have such a nice tan, and your hair turns "beach bum" blonde. You are a cutie!

(TIP)
COMBINE TEXTURES AS WELL AS COLORS

FABRIC FRAMES

c o n t r a s t

Young and old. Fair and roughened. This photograph initially simply meant to capture a grandfather-granddaughter moment, it came to represent more to me. I leapt out at me as representative of an age contrast, a contrast of experience, of differences. I looked at Alayna's fair skin, her unblemished complexion, then at my father's own skin, marked by years of hard work, outdoor exposure, time. A photographic contrast, captured here innocently, unplanned. Those are the best kind of photographs, the ones that delight me with surprise when I see them in their full glory, as if I had never seen them before.. This one to me, speaks of age, of change, of wisdom, of contrast. A wise man, an innocent child, a passing of torches, tender touches. Linkage, time and change. My thoughts, all from one photo.

(TIP)
SCRUNCH, BUNCH AND COMBINE FABRICS
FOR ONE-OF-A-KIND PHOTO MATTES

BEAUTIFUL BLOSSOMS

MAKE LOVELY PHOTO MATTES

SO BLESSED TO BE SISTERS BY MELLETTE BEREZOSKI

So blessed to be sisters

We talk on the phone for hours.
We cry to each other and are there for each other.
We have many, many inside jokes.
We can poke fun at ourselves
but can still have deep conversations about life.
We love each other's kids like they are our own.
We laugh until our sides hurt.
We are alike in some ways and different in others.
We are so incredibly blessed to be sisters.

Mellette and Winnie, September 2005

(TIP)

BORDER YOUR PHOTO
WITH FLOWERS, EITHER
IN FRONT OR PEEKING
OUT FROM BEHIND

RUB-ONS

REVEAL VISUAL TEXTURE, COLOR AND PERSONALITY

M BY MAGGIE HOLMES

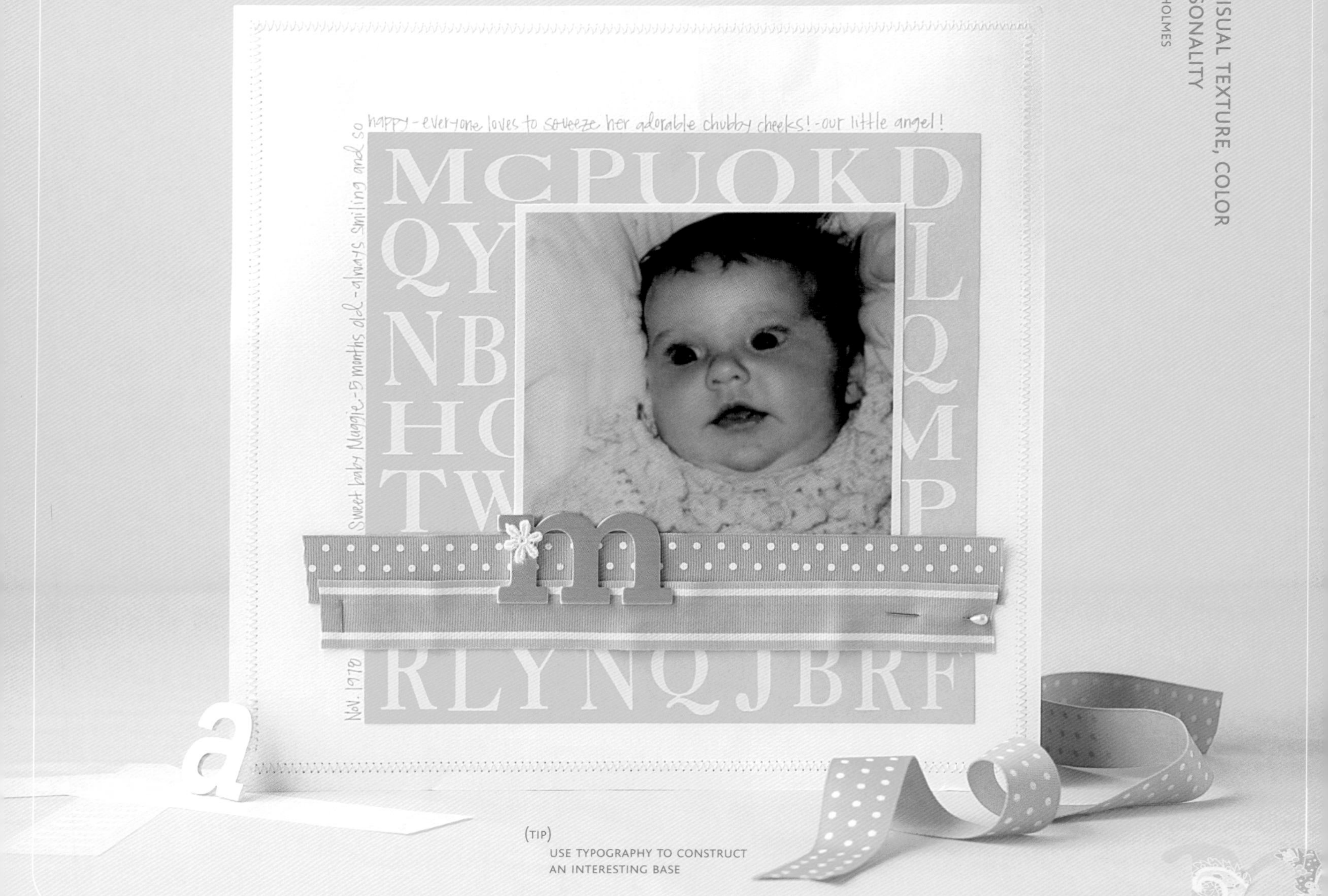

Sweet baby Maggie-5 months old-always smiling and so happy-everyone loves to squeeze her adorable chubby cheeks!-our little angel!
MCPUOKD
QY L
NB Q
HC M
TW P
m
RLYNQJBRF
Nov. 1970

(TIP)

USE TYPOGRAPHY TO CONSTRUCT AN INTERESTING BASE

WORK WITH PLENTIFUL SELECTIONS
FOR YOUR BACKGROUND

LUCKY BY MAGGIE HOLMES

I feel so lucky to be the mother of these adorable & sweet boys! They are more than I ever dreamed of! Sept 2005

(TIP)

STRIKING PAPERS CAN PUNCH-UP
THE IMPACT OF YOUR PHOTOS

PAINT METAL

CONSTRUCT NOTEWORTHY MATTES

EIGHT BY KRIS STANGER

(TIP)

DISTRESS AND PAINT MOULDING
STRIPS TO MATCH YOUR PHOTOS

INTERLACE RIBBONS

my 2 sons

blessed, grateful, thankful
for my 2 sons...

Okay,
have m
I know
My favo
I think

(TIP)
COMBINE RIBBONS AND LACE FOR A SOFT VINTAGE LOOK

METAL MESH

(TIP)

COMBINE RIBBON AND METAL
FOR AN ECLECTIC STYLE

relax

discover

HERE you are in your shades, taking a moment and just relaxing. You have so much ahead of you. I know you are the type of person who naturally takes on a lot. Volunteer work, club activities, and personal hobbies. I just want to make sure you take these moments for yourself. To know that it's okay to slow down. You have a lot of time later to be an adult, so for now breathe deep. Relax. Enjoy.

PHOTOGRAPHY IS A HUGE PASSION OF MINE. HUGE! IT HAS BEEN EVER SINCE I CAN REMEMBER. FROM
THE TIME I WAS FOURTEEN YEARS OLD I'VE HAD A CAMERA OF MY OWN. AND IF THE CAMERA BROKE,
GOT LOST, STOLEN, (OR LET'S SAY A FRIEND SPILLED POP ON IT... HYPOTHETICALLY SPEAKING, OF
COURSE) THE FOLLOWING CHRISTMAS, A NEW CAMERA WOULD BE THE FIRST THING ON MY LIST. AND
DAD ALWAYS WENT ABOVE & BEYOND TO MAKE SURE IT WAS A QUALITY CAMERA. SOMETHING THAT
WOULD ALLOW ME TO CONTINUE THIS PASSION OF MINE; *documenting life through photos.* IN JUST
OVER THE LAST TEN YEARS I THINK I'VE GONE THROUGH FOUR CAMERAS AND AM VERY HAPPILY IN
LOVE WITH CAMERA NUMBER FIVE! MY FIRST DIGITAL CAMERA AND THE FIRST I'VE PURCHASED
MYSELF; A CANON DIGI-REBEL SLR. I LOVE IT! AND NEEDLESS TO SAY, I TAKE IT WITH ME ALMOST
EVERYWHERE I GO. (LIKE ALL OF THE CAMERAS THAT CAME BEFORE IT.) ANXIOUS TO GET THE NEXT
GREAT PHOTO OF MY FAMILY, MY FRIENDS, MY LIFE. A PHOTOGRAPH FILLED WITH EMOTION & MEMORY.
PHOTOGRAPHY IS A SERIOUS LOVE OF MINE AND ALWAYS HAS BEEN. A HUGE PART OF MY LIFE;
EVIDENT IN THE PHOTOS ABOVE OF ME, TAKING PHOTOS OF MY FRIENDS JESSI STRINGHAM &
SHANNON MONTEZ; AND THEN ME & FRIEND, ELSIE FLANNIGAN, TAKING PHOTOS OF A GROUP OF
...-PROVO. *Both were taken in August of 2005.*

(TIP)
USE DOUBLE-SIDED TAPE
TO CATCH THE GLITTER

VELLUM LAYERS

SEE-THROUGH SHEETS FORM
UNDERSTATED SOPHISTICATION

9 THINGS ABOUT ME BY LONI STEVENS

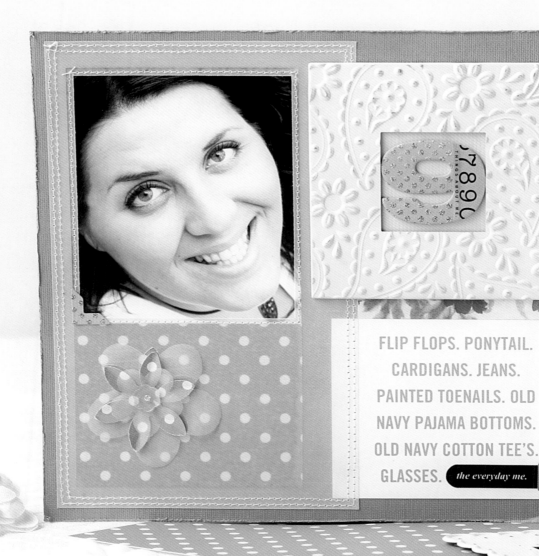

FLIP FLOPS. PONYTAIL.
CARDIGANS. JEANS.
PAINTED TOENAILS. OLD
NAVY PAJAMA BOTTOMS.
OLD NAVY COTTON TEE'S.
GLASSES. *the everyday me.*

(TIP)
VELLUM IS SUBTLE YET DESIGN-WORTHY WHEN LAYERED OVER BACKGROUNDS

CHIPBOARD TITLES

PHOTO CORNERS

GAMEBOARD ALPHAS

QUICK RUB-ONS

FOAM STAMPS

ACRYLIC COLOR

COMPUTER FONTS

HANDWRITING

LAYER RUB-ONS

SUSPENDED LETTERS

FABRIC PHRASES

STITCHED WORDAGE

4
TITLES & WORDAGE

(TIP)

USE A CONTRASTING COLOR
FOR TITLE AND EMBOSS

PHOTO CORNERS

NAUGHTY NEWT BY MAGGIE HOLMES

TITLE AROUND EDGES OF LARGE PICTURES

(TIP)

USE DIFFERENT STYLES AND
COLORS OF LETTER STICKERS

GAMEBOARD ALPHAS

I try my best to keep Daisy entertained and happy, but sometimes it's hard! Shannon and I took our kids to the zoo and thought they would have a blast. Unfortunately, it was so hot that we got lots of comments like "I'm dying!" and "It's too hot to be at the zoo today!". Oh well. They actually did have a good time, when they weren't busy complaining. Silly kids!!

OCCASION: San Antonio Zoo
DATE: July 2005
NOTES: HOT !!

Tired, and ready to go...

(TIP) ADD PAPER OR PAINT TO DECORATE DIMENSIONAL CHIPBOARD

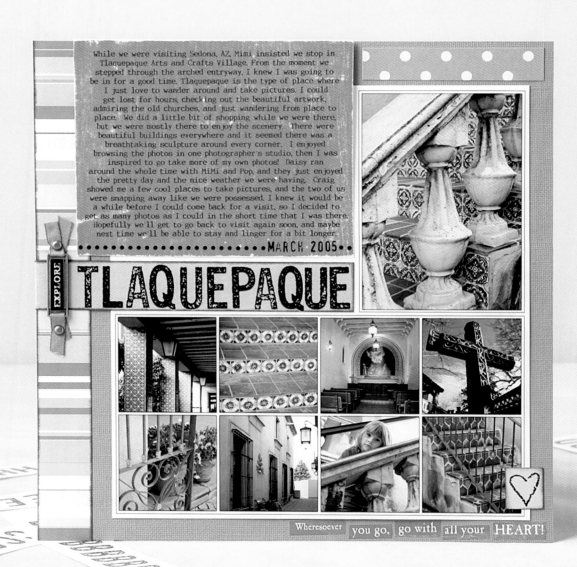

While we were visiting Sedona, AZ, Mimi insisted we stop in Tlaquepaque Arts and Crafts Village. From the moment we stepped through the arched entryway, I knew I was going to be in for a good time. Tlaquepaque is the type of place where I just love to wander around and take pictures. I could get lost for hours, checking out the beautiful artwork, admiring the old churches, and just wandering from place to place. We did a little bit of shopping while we were there, but we were mostly there to enjoy the scenery. There were beautiful buildings everywhere and it seemed there was a breathtaking sculpture around every corner. I enjoyed browsing the photos in one photographer's studio, then I was inspired to go take more of my own photos! Daisy ran around the whole time with MiMi and Pop, and they just enjoyed the pretty day and the nice weather we were having. Craig showed me a few cool places to take pictures, and the two of us were snapping away like we were possessed. I knew it would be a while before I could come back for a visit, so I decided to get as many photos as I could in the short time that I was there. Hopefully we'll get to go back to visit again soon, and maybe next time we'll be able to stay and linger for a bit longer.

•MARCH 2005•

EXPLORE TLAQUEPAQUE

Wheresoever you go, go with all your HEART!

(TIP)
FOR CUSTOM-MADE TITLES, USE A VARIETY OF COMBINED RUB-ONS

(TIP)

STAMPING ON TRANSPARENCIES ALLOWS
YOU TO TRY IT UNTIL YOU LIKE IT

ACRYLIC COLOR

APPLY PAINT DIRECTLY ONTO FOAM STAMPS

CARD **PARTY** BY LYNNE MONTGOMERY

(TIP)
STAMP RIGHT ONTO YOUR PROJECTS

Becca is so darn cute when I pull out the camera. She immediately starts to ham things up for me and says, "You can take my picture." S[...] and Daisy will often argue over who gets to be in front of the camera and over who looks silliest in each photo. We took these pictures one night out at the softball field. The girls played for about an hour and a half and we hid under the tent when a storm blew past. It felt great out there—one of the coolest nights of the summer! Afterwards, we watched Chris play his 2 games and the girls cheered him on. They found some boys to chase around and they ran after them for half the night. By the time the game ended, they were a dirty, happy mess!

(TIP)

USING COMPUTER FONTS, TITLE DIRECTLY ONTO YOUR PHOTOS

HANDWRITING

Let it...

SNOW

Let it snow... let it snow...

This year, the SNOW came much later than usual, and Grace was getting IMPATIENT! She would watch out her bedroom window, waiting for the SNOWFLAKES to fall to the ground.

LET IT SNOW

(TIP)
COMBINE HANDWRITING WITH OTHER ELEMENTS
SUCH AS RUB-ONS, COMPUTER TEXT OR STAMPING

LAYER RUB-ONS

CREATE A TIERED TITLE

HARPER KATE BY JOANNA BOLICK

How quickly we have come to know you, little one. Your softness, your sweetness, and even your grumpiness! It's hard to believe that you've been in our lives for just 7 short weeks! 9.14.05

HARPER *Kate*

(TIP)

OVERLAP OR LAYER RUB-ONS, STICKERS AND TITLE BOXES FOR A BOLSTERED EFFECT

SUSPENDED LETTERS

CREATE A PAGE TITLE USING RIBBON, BRADS AND SAFETY PINS AS ANCHORS

SANTA COLE BY JOANNA BOLICK

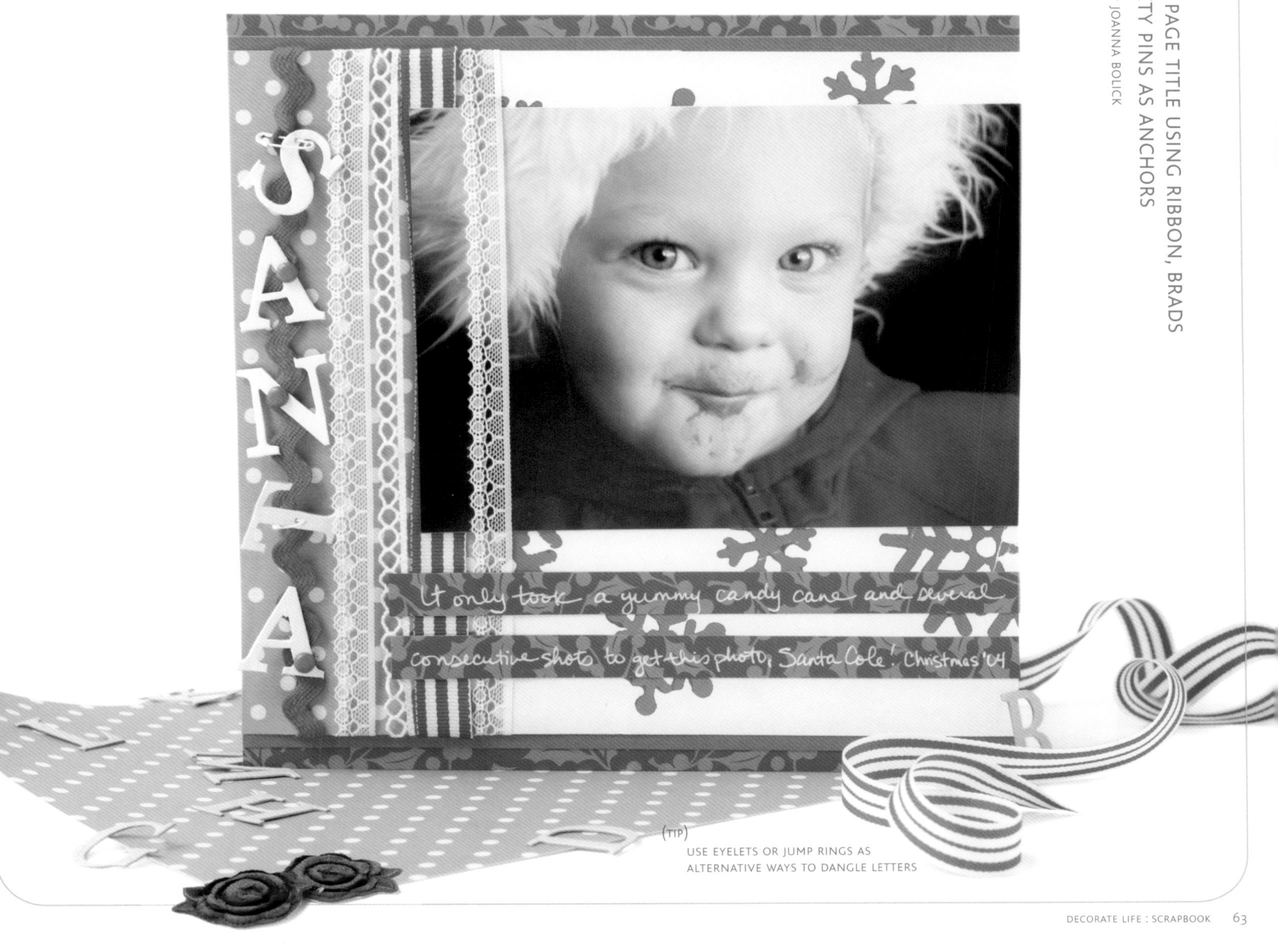
SANTA
It only took a yummy candy cane and several
consecutive shots to get this photo, Santa Cole! Christmas '04

(TIP)
USE EYELETS OR JUMP RINGS AS ALTERNATIVE WAYS TO DANGLE LETTERS

STITCHED WORDAGE

ACCENTS CONTRIBUTE HOMESPUN CHARM

MY FRIEND PAIGE BY KRIS STANGER

(TIP)
SEW THROUGH RUB-ONS, STICKERS AND MORE WHILE
EXPERIMENTING WITH DIFFERENT STITCH TECHNIQUES

VINTAGE TOUCH

ALPHABET ACCENTS

CREATIVE MONOGRAMS

USING TABS

LABEL HOLDERS

FLOWER ARRANGEMENTS

A THROUGH Z

RIBBON PRINT

VERTICAL TITLES

DIFFERENT SHADES

METAL MAKEOVER

CUSTOM CORNERS

CHANGED HEART

ALTERED GAMEBOARD

PAINT EMBELLISHMENTS

MINIATURE FRAMES

RESOURCEFUL RIBBON

STITCHED TAGS

5
EMBELLISHMENTS

VINTAGE TOUCH

CLASSIC EMBELLISHMENTS
I LOVE YOU BY MARIA GRACE ABUZMAN

touch (tuch) 1. to feel 2. come in physical contact 3. the sense in which physical items are felt

adore (e·dor) to glorify or worship 2. treasure or cherish 3. to love deeply

togetherness (to geth ur nes) the spending of much time together, resulting in a more unified and stable relationship

cherish (cher ish) 1. to hold dear; treasure 2. to care for; treat with great care

romantic (ro man tik) 1. fanciful or fictitious 2. swept up in passion and enchantment

I Love You

(TIP)
USE DECORATIVE-EDGED SCISSORS
FOR EYE-CATCHING CUTS

ALPHABET ACCENTS

CREATE TITLES WITH GAMEBOARD LETTERS

JH BY MARIA GRACE ABUZMAN

(TIP)
TUCK BLOSSOMS INSIDE LABEL HOLDERS

ATTACH WITH RIBBON

SERIOUSLY SILLY BY LYNNE MONTGOMERY

SILLY

SWEET & SASSY

Skye Simms 2005

(TIP)
USE ACRYLIC PAINT FOR CUSTOM COLOR

Victory
emerge as champion

commitment

practice

success

As I sat in the stands at 7:00 am and watched your first day of swim team practice and saw all the laps you were swimming, I really felt for you. I know how strenuous it is because I started swimming laps for exercise a few months ago and I remember feeling like I was going to die after only one lap. I was breathing 10 times harder than I do when I run. It was so exhausting. Slowly but surely I've built up my endurance and now can swim 40 laps.

I could tell by watching you that you weren't having the best time. After practice you walked over to me and "tossed" or should I say "threw" your goggles at me and exclaimed how much you hated it and how you weren't coming back and no one could make you. Ooh this created a problem I thought. I really wanted you to have this experience, but I also knew I could not make you go. I had also volunteered to be the neighborhood car pool and had made commitments to take others. I didn't want to disappoint them by backing out. I wondered what to do. How could I get you to want to go? Not to mention it was such a bargain experience for only $35.00.

I began by telling you that this (your first day) was the hardest day and each day to come would be a little easier. I told you that your endurance would be strengthened daily, and if you kept at, eventually you wouldn't have a problem keeping up with the workouts. We talked about giving up and sticking it out. All the other times you've tried something new you've always stuck it out and have been proud of your accomplishments. Baseball wasn't easy when you first started and neither was soccer but look how you love those games now. You're signed up for football this Fall. Just think of how well conditioned you'll be from swimming all Summer. You'll be one step ahead of the game. Living in Arizona I talked to you about how swimming is something you'll do for the rest of your life. Even though soccer, baseball, football, etc. are all fun, people usually don't do those things as adults. But swimming is something you will always do and it's important to be an excellent swimmer.

Well, I wasn't getting much response one way or the other. But we had these conversations throughout the day. I invited you to come and watch me swim along with my neighbor Karen Simms the next morning at our community pool. You were excited about that and sat and watched as we swam. Karen had gone to college on a swim scholarship and swims like an olympic swimmer. I on the other hand do not do flip turns and such but can hold my own without embarrassment. That same morning another friend's husband, Terry Gooch was also there. He was swimming laps training for a mini triathalon. I think seeing these adults who are part of your life, who you know and trust, actually doing the thing that is being asked of you made a huge impact on you. I wasn't just telling you to do something but I was doing it myself. After we got home from my workout you were ready to go to yours. You never complained once since. You earned many ribbons, and although you were no where near the fastest swimmer on your team, I know you felt a huge since of accomplishment. Who wouldn't after accomplishing the most difficult thing they'd ever done. You see, it's not about winning but about trying and finishing. Now you can swim a whopping 56 laps!! Way to go!!

(TIP)
YET ANOTHER USE FOR METAL RIMMED TAGS

LABEL HOLDERS

(TIP)

INCORPORATE ALPHABET RUB-ONS TO HIGHLIGHT KEY WORDS

FLOWER ARRANGEMENTS

PAINT CHIPBOARD BLOSSOMS

A CRAZY GOOD TIME BY LONI STEVENS

[a crazy good time.]

[with crazy cool girls.]

TWO GOOD FRIENDS I MET THROUGH SCRAPBOOKING, MAGGIE HOLMES & ROBYN WERLICH. SUCH COOL CHICKS! ALL THREE OF US LIVE IN UTAH, SO WHEN THE OPPORTUNITY PRESENTS ITSELF TO GET TOGETHER... WE'RE ALL OVER IT. THESE PHOTOS WERE TAKEN OUTSIDE OF PEBBLES (A SCRAPBOOK STORE IN OREM) DURING CKU-PROVO. ROBYN WAS UP FROM ST. GEORGE TAKING CKU-ALBUMS, SO THURSDAY NIGHT MAGGIE DROVE DOWN FROM SOUTH JORDAN AND ALL THREE OF US, AND MY FRIEND KERRI, MET UP FOR DINNER AT THE CALIFORNIA PIZZA KITCHEN, INSIDE UNIVERSITY MALL. KERRI HAD TO GET HOME AFTER DINNER, BUT MAGGIE, ROBYN AND I WENT TO PEBBLES AND DID SOME SHOPPING. OH, GOOD TIMES! WE SPENT A GOOD CHUNK OF TIME AFTERWARDS IN THE PARKING LOT JUST TALKING, LAUGHING AND TAKING PHOTOS (BEING DORKS). WE GOT LAUGHING SO HARD WHEN THE CAMERA CAME OUT, IT WAS FUN. I LOVE SPENDING TIME WITH THESE GIRLS. **August 4, 2005**

(TIP)
SECURE MULTIPLE FLOWERS TO PAPER AND
PAINT ALL AT ONCE INSTEAD OF INDIVIDUALLY

JOY

JOY

JOY

JOY

There is no greater Joy in life, than to be loved
unconditionally

(TIP)
MIX AND MATCH FONTS WITHIN A WORD FOR A FUNKY LOOK

re: **beautiful**

(Delicate, lovely to behold)

No. #2
little girl **beloved**

Addison

PRECIOUS (presh´·es) 1. of great worth 2. beloved; cherished

beautiful (byoot´·e-ful) 1. pleasingly attractive physical appearance 2. lovely; fine to behold 3. de

sweet is the sight of your smile -
Sweet is the sight of your small dancing feet, turning ever round & round -
sweet is the sight of your shining bright eyes, even as they glow with a hint of mischief-
sweet is your laughter - how I love that simple sound
.... sweet you are... -my little girl

(TIP)
STITCH SMALLER RIBBON ONTO TEXTURED
BACKGROUND FOR OUTSTANDING DEPTH

VERTICAL TITLES

(TIP)

FOR A MORE PLEASING LAYOUT, LAYER DIFFERENT RUB-ONS

How do you enjoy
your day?

By gracing it with a
smile, enjoying the
sun, and laughing
out loud.

(TIP) CHOOSE A BASIC SHAPE AND USE
THROUGHOUT YOUR PAGE

TRANSFORM FRAMES INTO PHOTO ACCENTS

NANA AND KAITLYN BY LORI BERGMANN

(TIP)
PAINT IN LAYERS, ADDING COLOR VARIATION TO METAL

CUSTOM CORNERS

CUT UP METAL FRAMES AND DISTRESS

WHO, WHAT, WHEN, WHERE? BY LORI BERGMANN

(TIP)
CURVE SHARP EDGES OF METAL
CORNERS BY GENTLY TAPPING
WITH HAMMER

WHO am I, really?
WHAT makes me
truly happy?
WHERE wie
this time next y
WHEN will I n
to make a chang

So many questions!
But I know if I keep
doing the best I can
& live each day to its
fullest, I will have
some great answers
soon! April 2005

GREAT FUN

FROLIC play

a family that plays together stays together

(TIP)

ALTER GAMEBOARD TO CREATE A CUSTOM EMBELLISHMENT

ALTERED GAMEBOARD

COVERED SURFACES

ANY OCCASION GIFT TAG SET BY MELLETTE BEREZOSKI

(TIP)

APPLY DIAMOND GLAZE FOR A GLASS-LIKE EFFECT

oh, baby

BABY

I must admit that being pregnant is not one of my favorite things... i can be pretty moody and irritable...and the last month seems to last forever. Luckily, the outcome is worth it

AUG 2005 ♥ 34 WEEKS PREGNANT WITH LILY ♥

motherhood

(TIP)
BRING ANY KIND OF EMBELLISHMENTS
INTO HARMONY WITH PAINT

SMALL PHOTOS PROVIDE
AN ADDITIONAL FOCAL POINT

TEENY TINY TOOTSIES BY JOANNA BOLICK

teeny, tiny, eeney, weeney,

soft, sweet and oh so adorable

10 little toes on 2 baby feet

I just can't get enough of you

TEENY TINY •
tootsies 8.20.05

(TIP) SCALE PHOTOGRAPHS FOR DIFFERENT EFFECTS

RESOURCEFUL RIBBONS

classiC chloe

it's a good thing aunt jenn has the skill
to be unnoticable
because it's this simple with Chloe...

She's uncooperative

-unposed
and finds photos
completely unnecessary.

looks can be deceiving...

(TIP)
SECURE YOUR PHOTOS WITH RIBBON KNOTS

CURL Y Q

Kylie ...our little girl with curls

(TIP)
INCORPORATE DIFFERENT SIZES AND
TEXTURES INTO LAYOUT WITH VARYING TAGS

INTERACTIVE NARRATIVE

MEMORIES UNFOLD

COMMUNICATING STRIPS

TRANSPARENT BEAUTY

JOURNALING BLOCKS

TELLING TAGS

EFFECTIVE ENVELOPES

STAMPED BULLETS

DOOR TO DOOR

HIDDEN POCKETS

PHOTOGRAPHIC MEMORY

COMBINATION TECHNIQUES

6
JOURNALING

(TIP)
OTHERS CAN INTERACT BY PULLING ITEMS FROM
POCKETS AND OPENING MINIBOOKS OR FLAPS

MEMORIES UNFOLD

ADD HIDDEN JOURNALING

MIRACLE BY SHERELLE CHRISTENSEN

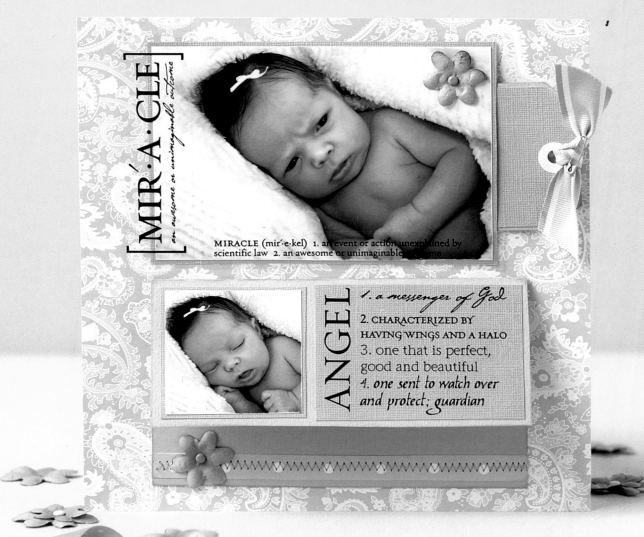

[MIR·A·CLE]
an awesome or unimaginable outcome

MIRACLE (mir´·e·kel) 1. an event or action unexplained by
scientific law 2. an awesome or unimaginable outcome

ANGEL
1. *a messenger of God*
2. CHARACTERIZED BY
HAVING WINGS AND A HALO
3. one that is perfect,
good and beautiful
4. *one sent to watch over
and protect; guardian*

(TIP)
SHARE EVEN MORE REMEMBRANCES WITH SIMPLE, FOLDED CARDSTOCK

COMMUNICATING STRIPS

WHY IS IT THAT I ALWAYS END UP

WITH ONE OF THESE TIGHT-LIPPED,

"TOUGH GUY" LOOKS WHENEVER

I AIM THE CAMERA TOWARDS A

YOUNGER BROTHER? A GUY THING?

BOYS
will be boys

(TIP)
PRINT ON LINEN OR TEXTURED CARDSTOCK
FOR A PROFESSIONAL APPEARANCE

TRANSPARENT BEAUTY

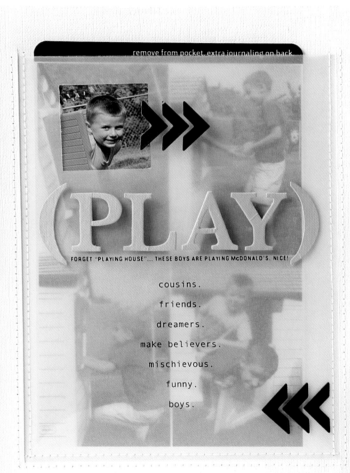

7.22.05

remove from pocket, extra journaling on back

(PLAY)

FORGET "PLAYING HOUSE"... THESE BOYS ARE PLAYING MCDONALD'S. NICE!

cousins.

friends.

dreamers.

make believers.

mischievous.

funny.

boys.

(TIP)
CREATE POUCHES TO ADD EXTRA JOURNALING
OR PHOTOS TO THE BACK OF PULLOUT

SOCCER dad

Joe is coaching Dayton's soccer team this year. He is so good with young kids. He is very encouraging and enthusiastic.

He teaches them drills and basic skills, does cheers with them, and makes sure they are all laughing & having a fun time.

Dayton loves that his daddy is his coach. He truly enjoys soccer practice & games, especially with his daddy by his side.

success

USE FRAMES TO HIGHLIGHT JOURNALING INSTEAD OF PHOTOS

SOCCER DAD BY MELLETTE BEREZOSKI

(TIP)

ADHERE FRAMES WITH FOAM TAPE FOR ADDED DIMENSION

H3

dream big

Over the years I have enjoyed driving some interesting sports cars. As I got older, I moved into SUV's, the latest being a Land Rover Discovery. My dream has always been to own a HUMMER, but beyond my car budget.

After admiring the Hummer I & II as they passed me on the highway or I saw them on the car lots, I was excited to see an advertisement for a new, smaller, more economical HUMMER III.

Soon after, on a visit to Oregon to visit my husband's son and family, we all drove into Portland to visit a dealership that carried HUMMERS. Of course we all loved the new H3 but no one purchased one.

A few days after arriving home Alec, my husbands son, called. I told him that I had found the prices of some of the chrome extras for the H3. We talked about the chrome gas tank cover. He said "We have that on ours."

At that point, I jokingly didn't want to talk to him and handed the phone over to my husband. After that, my husband said that I pouted around for a few days to the point that he felt obligated to take a trip to Sacramento to the HUMMER dealership.

The rest is history. In less than 2 ½ hours, we purchased my DREAM CAR, traded in our Land Rover and were on our way home. We didn't even have to leave the showroom floor, thank goodness, since the temperature was 103. I feel like I'm driving a beautiful piece of sculputre.

(TIP)
BREAK JOURNALING UP INTO MULTIPLE SECTIONS FOR AN EASIER READ

EFFECTIVE ENVELOPES

quirky

Snowball

cute

Cats leave
paw prints in our
hearts

(TIP)

KEEP YOUR REFLECTIONS PRIVATE BY
INSERTING THEM IN AN ENVELOPE

INTERESTING DESIGNS AND WORD STAMPS
CREATE FAST JOURNALING OPTIONS

ASHLEY BY LORI BERGMANN

NAME ASHLEY

BOX NUMBERS 1 2 3

discover

Life

explore

[ad·ven´·ture]

experience

September 2004

GRAND TOTAL

(TIP)

IF USING MULTIPLE PAINT COLORS ON A FOAM STAMP, APPLY
THE COLOR YOU WANT TO SHOW THROUGH THE MOST, LAST

beauty
bloom where you are planted.

2006
my love of flowers.
details enclosed.

Lift flap.

(TIP)
CUT YOUR PAGE PROTECTOR TO WORK WITH YOUR INTERACTIVE PAGE
AND MACHINE STITCH THE TOP CLOSED, ONCE LAYOUT IS INSIDE

HIDDEN POCKETS

STOW PHOTOGRAPHS AND MEMENTOS

BABY AIDEN BY KIMBERLY BEE

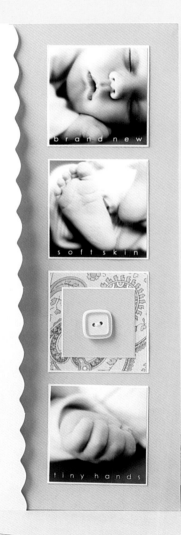

brand new

soft skin

tiny hands

newborn baby aiden

December 7, 2004

(TIP) CREATE A DECORATIVE FOLDER FOR YOUR TREASURES

PHOTOGRAPHIC MEMORY

Nathan **aka**

nate
nafers
punkin eater
punkinoots
sweet pea
nafanoots
chubba bubba
punkinooters
nafan
little heart sweet

(TIP)
RUB-ONS CAN ALSO BE USED FOR JOURNALING
ON A TRANSPARENCY, THEN LAYERED OVER PHOTO

COMBINATION TECHNIQUES

You radiate and shine and I'm so proud to call you my friend.

delight (di·lit) 1. to give great pleasure 2. to rejoice, or be highly pleased fun (fun) 1. lively, joyous inspire (in·spir) 1. to stimulate or impel. as to some creative effort 2. to motivate as by divine influence bright (brit) 1. shining with light

You're all this and more.

(TIP)
INCORPORATE DIFFERENT FLOW
PATTERNS FOR ADDED VISUAL FUN

CREATIVE CROPPING

PAPER BINDING

SINGULAR COLOR

MONOCHROMATIC

QUADRATIC EQUATION

SAME DIFFERENCE

STRONG COLORS

TIN FRAMES

7
MIX IT UP

CREATIVE CROPPING

PHOTOS IN NARROW STRIPS ADD DRAMA

FAMILY BY MELLETTE BEREZOSKI

The Berezoski Family. Squeezing into our bed for Friday night movie marathons Scouring thrift shops for hidden treasures. Making grocery shopping a family event. Taking long neighborhood walks. Talking Debating Sometimes arguing Laughing Crying Sometimes annoying each other But hugs are plentiful in this family And smothering cheeks with kisses is the norm Family It's what we do.

FAMILY

(TIP)
STAGGER CLOSE-UP FACIAL PHOTOS FOR VISUAL INTEREST

PAPER BINDING

CHANGE IT UP WITH PAPER

SAFETY AND SECURITY BY JENNIFER JENSEN

oh happy day!
now let's eat cake!!

second birthday

a daddy & a daughter
nothing like it in this world...

with her daddy

(TIP)
UTILIZE YOUR PAPER SCRAPS

SINGULAR COLOR

STICK TO AN INDIVIDUAL TONE

GYM SHOES BY ERIN TERRELL

A LOOK LIKE THIS BY ERIN TERRELL

I love you more than my...

"I love you more than my gym shoes." Super silly, but I say it to Daisy all the time. Blame it on Grammy...she started it years ago by telling Daisy, "I love you more than my suitcase". Daisy then started telling me that she loved me more than her suitcase, imitating what her Grammy told her. Pretty soon, instead of saying a plain old "I love you", we all started picking random objects around the house that we loved each other "better than".
We discovered it's an easy way to tell someone we love them when we're out in public without sounding too serious. Plus, it's good for laughs! So, when I tell Daisy, "I love you more than my gym shoes" or Chris says, "I love you more than fish", we may sound a little silly...but it's our own secret way of saying that we think that certain someone is pretty special! And Daisy, I want you to know. I really do love you more than my stinky gym shoes!

GYM SHOES ????????

XO XO

It's pretty hard to resist...

I happen to think Savanna is one of the most beautiful babes I've ever seen--and I'm not just partial to her because she's a relative. Maybe I'm a bit partial simply because she reminds me a lot of Daisy. Those sweet little baby cheeks and her huge blue eyes just get to me every time! She is stunning!! She lives in South Carolina, so I've only gotten to see her twice. Daisy loves when we get to go and visit her and always asks when she is going to see her again. We just can't get enough of cute little Savanna! I snapped these pictures in December of 2004 when we were visiting for Christmas. We probably won't be able to see her again until next Christmas when she's another year older. That's ok because she'll probably have even more personality then she does now. That's one of the best things about her--she's always full of smiles and just radiates happiness.

a LOOK LIKE THIS. Savanna

Super Sweet Thing

(TIP)
PLAY WITH OPACITY TO MAKE TYPE STAND OUT

MONOCHROMATIC

BLEND ONE CORE COLOR FAMILY

HAPPY 2005 BY LYNNE MONTGOMERY

TRADITION 2005 BY LYNNE MONTGOMERY

(TIP)

CHOOSE SOLID COLORS DIRECTLY FROM PATTERNED PAPER

QUADRATIC EQUATION

DIVIDE LAYOUT INTO FOUR SECTIONS FOR PHOTOS AND JOURNALING

THAT CRAZY SILLY GOOFY WACKY HAT BY SHERELLE CHRISTENSEN

That CRAZY... silly... goofy... WACKY...

HAT

this CRAZY cow-print HAT drove me crazy when my little sister wore it, and LUCKY ME! my mom sent it home with my KIDS! Russell is such a WACKY guy.... he always wears the HAT all around while he PLAYS... especially when riding WHINNIE the WONDER HORSE!

Russell SEP 2005 2 years old

(TIP)

PAGE CAN BE DRESSED UP OR DOWN
BY CHOOSING MORE ELEGANT OR
FUNKY EMBELLISHMENTS

just us...

GIRLS
GIRLS
girls

♥ on September 27th, we welcomed a ♥ sweet BABY GIRL into our home. GRACE was so excited to have a little SISTER of her own! She has lots of plans for LILY... playing DOLLS and POLLY POCKETS, dressing up and much more. It is going to be fun with another GIRL!

Mommy, Grace
SEP 2005
and Lily...

SAME DIFFERENCE

USE IDENTICAL PAGE DESIGNS WITH DIFFERENT COLOR SCHEMES

2 DEVOTED BY LONI STEVENS

2 PERSONALITIES BY LONI STEVENS

(TIP)
IF YOU HAVE A HARD TIME VISUALIZING THE DESIGN
WITH COLOR PHOTOS, TRY USING BLACK AND WHITE

ALOHA STYLE BY MARIA GRACE ABUZMAN

THE HAPPY GRAD BY MARIA GRACE ABUZMAN

aloha
STYLE

Julie took to Hawaii really well. Even though we were all there for Helery's wedding, that didn't stop Julie from enjoying the full aloha experience. On the night of the luau, she waited in line a long time just to get a hibiscus "tattoo." Julie was so proud of that little flower and here she is showing it off with style. It truly was an excellent memento from a fabulous trip.

the happy
GRAD

Graduation day! I'm so proud of Divine. So glad I was able to come down to celebrate with her. We've been friends for a long time and each step she takes in life, I feel as if I'm right there with her. And on this day, as Divine was awarded her Masters, I couldn't have been more proud. So in true graduation style, she put on her shades and her congratulatory lei and smiled wide for her big day.

celebrate...

(TIP)
ADAPT THE SAME LAYOUT DESIGN TO DIFFERENT OCCASIONS BY SWITCHING AROUND COLORS

TIN FRAMES

CREATE LARGE PHOTO CORNERS

LET THE JOURNEY BEGIN BY JOANNA BOLICK

The last stop on our Italian vacation was Venice. Enchanting, unique, historic, floating Venice, full of bridges, water, and boats. We splurged and used our last 50 Euros for a short gondola ride, knowing that we would most likely not be returning to this city again. We enjoyed drifting through alleyways amongst the city and listening to the gondolier share the history of this place. The sunset on this particular day reflected not only the close of day but also signaled the end of our trip as well. We were travel weary and cold, happy to be returning home, and filled with memories spent exploring new places together and enjoying each other's company.

March 11, 2005

LET THE *Journey* BEGIN

Harper Kate, we love you so! You have quickly become an integral part of our family. We can't ever imagine what we did without you in our lives. You are cute, sweet, adorable, gassy, happy, cranky, loud and loveable! Here you are at just 4 weeks of age, already looking at the camera like a pro! We love you so, sweet girl! xo

Simply IRRESISTABLE

WHAT COULD BE BETTER THAN PLAYING AT THE BEACH? THIS YEAR MARKED YOUR 3RD TRIP TO NORTH MYRTLE BEACH, AND THIS TIME AROUND YOU SHOWED MORE INTEREST IN YOUR SURROUNDINGS — YOU WATCHED PAWPAW PULL FISH FROM THE OCEAN, EXCLAIMED WITH DELIGHT OVER MINNOWS, CRABS, AND SAND FLEAS, AND EXPLORED AND TENTATIVELY TOUCHED THE BUBBLY FOAM AND SMELLS THAT WASHED UP ON THE SAND. HOW WE LOVE TO WATCH YOU GROW AND EXPLORE THE WORLD, YOUNG ONE! MAY IT ALWAYS HOLD SUCH FASCINATION. JUNE 2005

OUTDOORS

(TIP)
FRAMES ARE THIN ENOUGH TO BE CAREFULLY CUT WITH SCISSORS

INSTRUCTIONS

SUPPLY LIST

GALLERY

ARTISTS

8
BOOK END

PAGES 10 - 11 LONI STEVENS

EIGHTIES CHILD

1. Using Photoshop Elements or a similar program, type up key words and print out
2. Print journaling on chipboard
3. Punch photo corners out of matching patterned paper

Petite signage, simply fabulous trims, charm and gem stickers (brooke): Making Memories

Computer font: Fabianestem and QuickType

Wood flower: Prima

Photo corner die-cut: QuicKutz

Other: chipboard and crystal

EXPLORE. THE JOY OF DISCOVERY

1. Arrange letter stickers on white cardstock
2. Soften the look by adding a sheet of vellum over the letters
3. Use rub-on words atop the vellum
4. Print journaling on a transparency and sew it down over the background using a sewing machine

Simply fabulous monogram alphas and trims (brooke), vintage hip buttons, rub-ons, rub-ons alphabet (circus) and rub-ons images (butterfly): Making Memories

Computer font: Avante Garde

Other: vellum and transparency

PAGES 12 MARIA GRACE ABUZMANN

EMILY

1. Cut solid pieces of paper to the desired size
2. Place solid papers on a background to determine placement
3. Adhere gingham ribbon horizontally and vertically along seams
4. Adhere polka dot ribbon on top of gingham ribbon
5. Embellish on top of cross section of ribbons

MM kids quilted stickers, trims and paper (bella), monograms (metal) and rub-ons images: Making Memories

+ VARIATION 1

1. Incorporate patterned paper into the same blocked layout

PAGES 13 LYNNE MONTGOMERY

THINGS I LOVE AT 5

1. Cut strips of patterned paper for the top and bottom section of the layout and adhere to solid background paper
2. Attach the striped ribbon, using an exacto knife to cut a small slit at the top and then at the bottom of the middle section where the patterned papers and solid papers meet
3. Adhere ric rac horizontally across the top and bottom where sections meet
4. Adhere alpha gameboard pieces for the title along with photos and embellished squares

MM kids paper and trims (bella), gameboard alphabet (sadie), eyelet charm tags, eyelet letter/number, metal rimmed tag, tiny alphas, rub-ons mini, cardstock tags, brads from attachment assortment, charmed words and charmed: Making Memories

Stamp pad: Psx rubber stamps

Other: paint chips and personal memorabilia

PAGE 14 JOANNA BOLICK

MAYDAY

1. Trim edges of paisley paper and position over purple cardstock
2. Accordion-fold a lightweight fabric and adhere to the page with staples (hidden beneath the pleats)
3. Add photos
4. Print journaling on cardstock and position between fabric folds
5. Pin a small swatch of fabric behind calling card and adhere
6. Add ribbon and sticker title

Simply fabulous trims, paper (meg), velvet alphas and calling cards and vintage hip trinkets: Making Memories

Fabric: Laurie Smith Collection from Hancock Fabrics

Computer font: My Dear Watson

+ VARIATION 1

1. Cut a smaller portion of fabric and fray the edges
2. Adhere to page using brads
3. Pre-punching holes with small hole punch makes brad insertion easier

PAGE 15 ERIN TERRELL

FINDING LILLY

1. Add a strip of striped paper to your dotted background sheet after treating the edges with black ink
2. Add one medium (this will be your photo matte) and one smaller piece of paisley paper after treating the edges with black ink
3. Trim a file folder shape out of turquoise blue cardstock, ink the edges, place rub-ons alphabet on the tab, then place behind the upper left corner of the photo matte
4. Use a circle cutter to trim various sized circles out of striped paper, inking the edges and layering them over the smaller paisley paper strip
5. Add a rub-on title to turquoise blue cardstock, inking the edges and place in lower right hand corner for title
6. Set up photo in Photoshop, adding a border around it and type your journaling
7. Ink photo edges, cut a slit and slide ribbon and brads through, adhering them to the back
8. Add rub-ons to the turquoise cardstock to spell out "Lily," ink the edges and place over the ribbon

Simply fabulous embellishment papers, trims and brad accents (meg), black ink from distressing kit, staples and rub-ons alphabet (hudson): Making Memories

Rub-ons: Autumn Leaves (SuMaking Memories 2005 and puppy)

Basic grey rub-ons: Darling

Other: circle cutter and Adobe Photoshop CS

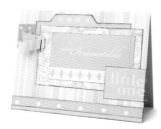

+ VARIATION 1

1. Layer calling card on top of paisley paper and layer that, in turn, on top of main card surface

2. Add file folder shaped cardstock behind the paisley paper followed by adding the rub-ons to cardstock and layering on page

3. Add solid and polka dot strips along bottom edge of card, staple a scrap of ribbon to upper left area of card, and finish off with daisy rub-ons at top of file folder

Simply fabulous embellishment paper (meg), trims (meg) and calling cards (all about me), vintage hip trims (paisley) and trinkets, black staples, black ink from distressing kit: Making Memories

Basic grey rub-ons: baby

PAGES 16 - 17 MELLETTE BEREZOSKI

BEAUTIFUL BRIDE

1. Trim cream cardstock to size

2. Use a ruler and pencil to lightly mark diagonal stitch lines

3. Machine stitch over markings and tape thread ends to back

4. Attach to solid meadow cardstock

Cardstock, patterned paper, rub-ons alphabet, vintage hip trims and trinkets, petals and brads: Making Memories

Photo corners: Kolo

Computer font: Avant Garde

Other: silk flower

MARRIED

1. Use a ruler and pencil to lightly mark off square stitch lines

2. Machine stitch over markings and tape thread ends to back

3. Attach to solid meadow cardstock

Cardstock, vintage hip paper (gracen), alphabet stickers, rub-ons wordage, blossoms, flower charm, ribbons, gameboard shapes (heart), photo flips and brads: Making Memories

Photo corners: Kolo and Canson

PAGE 18 KRIS STANGER

CAMRYN

1. Trim 9" x 9" floral paper, ⅛" on length and width

2. Place stickers until you are happy with the arrangement and adhere to floral paper

3. Lightly dry brush edges of scalloped and floral 9" x 9" paper as well as entire collage surface, using white paint

4. Fold a piece of 9" x 9" scalloped cardstock lengthwise and trim with scalloped scissors

5. Matte your photo on top surface and journal on inside

6. Run through printer before attaching for computer type journaling

7. Run photograph through printer to add name, then attach to cardstock and place onto 9" x 9" floral paper, backed by sherbet cardstock

8. Add embellishment trims and foam stamps

Scalloped sherbet paper, mini brads (flower), simply fabulous trims (brooke), basic white paint, rub-ons wordage (expressions), foam stamps (floral dingbat), like it is stickers (baby girl and girl): Making Memories

+ VARIATION 1

1. Layer stickers on top of paper and layer that, in turn, on top of main card surface

2. Using brad, adhere ribbon to card

3. Embellish with foam stamps and rub-ons

PAGE 19 JENNIFER JENSEN

HER PINK SHOES

1. Place three sheets of coordinating patterned paper on top of one another

2. Trace curved lines on the top sheet of paper

3. Cut along traced lines through all three sheets

4. For interest, choose different pieces of each patterned paper, then glue strips back together using a solid piece of contrasting cardstock

5. Leave a small space between each strip

Simply fabulous embellishment paper (maddi), rub-ons images (love), gameboard alphabet, rub-ons wordage and tiny alphas: Making Memories

Other: gem sticker

+ VARIATION 1

1. Using a paper trimmer, cut strips of varying width from patterned paper

2. Then, using a patterned piece of cardstock for background, glue cut strips of paper and ribbon to creat a new background

PAGES 22 - 23 JENNIFER JENSEN

AN ELEMENT OF CHILDHOOD

1. Create a non-stick edge on each sticker by lightly dusting the edge of your border stickers with baby powder

2. On the right edge of the page, overlap fractions of border stickers horizontally

3. Lightly sand the edges

4. Lift up the non-stick edges to give dimension

Vintage hip paper and borders (gracen) and trims (paisley), gameboard alphabet, red wagon and cardstock tags: Making Memories

+ VARIATION 1

1. Starting with the bottom piece of ribbon, stitch down to the background page

2. Place the next piece of ribbon on top of the bottom piece

3. Make sure the pieces are not aligned directly on top of one another, so you can still see the bottom layer

4. Stitch in place

5. Repeat again with the last piece of ribbon

6. Finish by placing a border sticker on top of the ribbon pieces

AN ELEMENT OF CHILDHOOD

1. Create a non-stick edge on each sticker by lightly dusting the edge of your border stickers with baby powder

2. On the right edge of the page, overlap four border stickers vertically

3. Lightly sand the edges

4. Lift up the non-stick edges to give dimension

Vintage hip paper and borders (gracen), gameboard alphabet and cardstock tags: Making Memories

PAGE 24 ERIN TERRELL

PATIENT MAN

1. In Photoshop, layout pictures with focal photo in color and the others in black and white

2. Fill background with light blue color and reduce opacity

3. Add title, decorative circles and merge all layers, adding a thin black border and print

4. Place photo on solid blue background and emboss a frame around it

5. Trim strips of teal green cardstock, miter the edges and place around the borders

6. Add trim along all border edges, using buttons to cover corners on all trims

7. Print and trim journaling into strips and place them in lower left corner of page

8. Finish by tying ribbon to 'little fish' tag and place on page

MM kids trims and accessory tags (ethan): Making Memories

PAGE 25 SHERELLE CHRISTENSEN

CHICKS

1. Layer different sized trims to create border

2. Use plenty of texture and color

3. Add a variety of trims such as lace, ribbon and ric rac

4. Paint chipboard letters and adhere for title

MM kid paper, quilted stickers and trims (ethan) and petals (spotlight mix): Making Memories

+ VARIATION 1

1. Add trim to everyday items such as zippers

2. Adhere to page vertically for an interesting border

PAGE 26 LORI BERGMANN

KAITLYN

1. Create a border of flower buttons, using floss to attach

2. Form curved cut between paper patterns by tracing a dinner plate

3. Dry brush photo matte using white paint

4. Give letter 'k' a dark pink base coat followed by a second coat of orange paint

5. Immediately wipe off last layer with a paper towel, revealing some pink

6. Dip opposite end of paint brush into paint and dab pink dots on to letter

7. Journal by hand on left side of page

Simply fabulous embellishment paper (maddi), MM kids buttons and trims, blossoms (wildflower spotlight), jigsaw alphabet (poolside), acrylic paint and rub-ons alphabet (heidi): Making Memories

+ VARIATION 1

1. Cut along the edge of the diamond patterned paper, silhouetting the diamond shape

2. Overlay onto striped paper

3. Add MM kids flower buttons and tie with floss at the diamond intersections

PAGE 27 JOY BOHON

TOOTHLESS-YOU

1. Make border by cutting a triangle template freehand

2. Align template with right hand side of your background, base of triangle flush with right hand side

3. After tracing, cut out triangle shapes from top to bottom of page

4. Cut smaller triangles and affix to the now vacant space to form the patterned border

5. Affix flowers to the tips of the border and add painted brads

6. Paint chipboard accents with acrylics and adhere title

7. Journaling is printed using textbox with colored fill

Simply fabulous embellishment paper (maddi), chipboard letters, gameboard alphabet (valentine), acrylic paint, blossoms and deco brads: Making Memories

Computer font: Century Schoolbook

+ VARIATION 1

1. Cut along the edge of the diamond patterned paper, silhouetting the diamond shape

2. Overlay onto striped paper

3. Add flower brads at the diamond intersections

PAGE 28 LYNNE MONTGOMERY

TALENTED '53

1. Take three file folders with a right, center and left tab, and stack them together, lining up the tabs

2. Make one vertical cut through the stack, leaving a strip that includes the tabbed portions

3. Using the three tabbed portions and the front portion, trace the four strips onto patterned paper

4. Cut the strips and distress by sanding, painting and inking and adhere the strips to your layout

5. Attach ribbon accent using brads and a paper piercer

6. Lay a strip of ribbon right side down in the desired place and pierce a hole through the ribbon and all four paper strip layers

7 Insert a brad and open on backside of layout to secure

8. Tie a knot in the ribbon and trim the edges

9. Complete steps six through ten for all three ribbon accents and rubber stamp wordage on tabs

Simply fabulous paper (brooke), vintage hip trims, brads and distressing kit: Making Memories

Vintage photo distress ink: Ranger

Rubber stamps: Psx

Computer font: Courier New

Other: buttons, ledger paper and old book paper

+ VARIATION 1

1. Trace the tabbed section of a file folder onto patterned paper two times, adding some length to fit your design size

2. Cut out shapes

3. Distress strips by sanding, painting and inking

4. Adhere strips to layout

5. Adhere velvet ribbon along the length of each strip, securing the ends with tiny brads

6. Stamp wordage onto tabs

PAGE 29 MARIA GRACE ABUZMAN

FAIRY PRINCESS

1. Use painted chipboard strips as borders on three sides of layout and distress

2. Use matching trims as border on remaining fourth side

---

3. Ink edges of photo corners and attach to upper corners of photograph

Simply fabulous embellishment paper and ribbon charms (brooke): Making Memories

PAGE 30 KRIS STANGER

LOVE AND ADORE YOU

1. Using a 1½" square punch, cut out opening

2. Dry brush over lavender paper and use foam stamps at top

3. Apply rub-ons directly over dry paint and embellish corner with ribbon

4. Glue hinges to border and add journaling underneath

Simply fabulous embellishment paper, trims and ribbon charms (meg), rub-ons wordage, foam stamps (floral dingbat) and photo flip: Making Memories

PAGE 31 MAGGIE HOLMES

FRIENDSHIP

1. Using scissors, create a scalloped border by cutting in a wave-like fashion back and forth

2. Choose the appropriate sized circle punch and punch holes inside of each scallop

3. Dry emboss circles onto the yellow cardstock with a Making Memories metal circle charm

Simply fabulous embellishment paper (meg), aquamarine velvet alpha, MM kids fresh stickers (bella), textured cardstock (polo club and spotlight) and foam stamps (valentine): Making Memories

PAGES 32 - 33 MELLETTE BEREZOSKI

LOVE YOU

1. Use rub-ons or type on paper, then use them to fill label holders

2. Connect label holders with ribbon

3. Add embellishments

Card, label holders, blossoms, woven ribbon, patterned paper and brads: Making Memories

LOVE ENDURES

1. Fill metal label holders with patterned paper, like it is stickers and small photo

2. Use different sized label holders in various shapes to add interest

3. Connect label holders with woven ribbon and attach to page

4. Secure ends of ribbon by taping to back

Cardstock, patterned paper, label holders, woven ribbon, petite signage, photo anchors, like it is stickers and brads: Making Memories

Computer font: Times New Roman by Microsoft Word

PAGES 34 - 35 KIMBERLY BEE

CLASSIC CUTIE

1. Divide layout into three sections

2. Title photo by printing or adding rub-ons

3. Adhere ribbon over section seams and finish with blossom embellishment

Blossoms (hydrangea) and ribbon: Making Memories

Other: paper

SOMETHING SPECIAL

1. Use patterned paper as background

2. Adhere photo

3. Use floss in colors found in patterned paper and braid

4. Adhere horizontally across seam

Simply fabulous embellishment paper (maddi), brads (flower) and eyelet alphabet: Making Memories

PAGES 38 - 39 LYNNE MONTGOMERY

CRAZY FOR YOU

1. Create the background tag from the vintage hip frame's cardboard packaging, apply walnut ink to cover paper and allow tag to dry

2. Glue inked paper to chipboard tag, let dry and trim excess paper off all edges

3. Stipple brown distress ink over entire surface, stamp wordage and add embellishments to front and message to back

Vintage hip frames, trinkets and trims, ribbon and rub-ons mini: Making Memories

GREAT MARRIAGE

1. Print quote on background paper

2. Piece together background papers and ric rac trim

3. Dip shipping tags in walnut ink for overall color and let dry

4. Stipple brown distress ink over tags and apply black ink around the edges

5. Wrap larger tags around main photo to matte

6. Add game pieces, cardstock tag and adhere to layout

7. Attach small photos to smaller tags, add embellishments and attach to layout with vintage hip buttons

Vintage hip paper and trims (gracen) and buttons (paisley), ribbon cards, black cardstock tags, naked line shipping tags, jump ring, shaped clip, mini brad, staple and black ink sponge: Making Memories

Game pieces: Li'l Davis

Walnut ink: Postmodern Design

Brown distress ink: Ranger

Rubber stamp: Hampton Art Stamps

+ VARIATION 1

1. Use ink to treat shipping tags and paper
2. Use same ink to stamp wordage
3. Cut the ends off of one side of paper so it resembles a tag shape
4. Mount photo onto tag, and finish by adding buttons and trim

PAGE 40 JENNIFER JENSEN

BE YOU

1. Place photo on scratch paper and brush paint onto foam stamps
2. Stamp all four sides of photo with foam stamps, so that half of stamp goes onto scratch paper (This creates a matte directly on the photo)
3. Create stitched photo matte by adhering photo onto background paper
4. Using a sewing machine, straight stitch around photo to create matte

Gameboard tags, rub-ons, blossoms, moxie fab stickers, vintage hip buttons, trims and border stickers (paisley), paper, foam stamps and acrylic paint: Making Memories

PAGE 41 KRIS STANGER

JULY 2004

1. Place four metal frames on cardstock, anchoring corners with glue dots
2. Wrap and knot twine at seams
3. Add 5" x 7" photograph and tags
4. Apply rub-ons directly onto metal frame

Vintage hip paper (paisley), metal frame, rub-ons (mixed muted) and naked line dyeable tags: Making Memories

+ VARIATION 1

1. Follow same layout concept as above, only adding flower brads at the seams

PAGE 42 JOY BOHON

CONTRAST 1 AND 67

1. Cut a lacy piece of fabric measuring a few inches longer on the bottom
2. Roll the excess fabric up manually and tie off sections with ribbon

Vintage hip paper (gracen), ribbon, washer words, acrylic paint, gameboard alphabet and jigsaw alphabet: Making Memories

Computer font: Dactylographe and Times New Roman

Other: fabric

+ VARIATION 1

1. Cut fabric to desired size and fray edges by pulling fabric apart at ends
2. Add brads at top of layout

PAGE 43 MELLETTE BEREZOSKI

SO BLESSED TO BE SISTERS

1. Punch flowers from red and pink coordinating papers
2. Randomly arrange flowers around photo and adhere
3. Add photo anchor and brad to one flower

Vintage hip paper, rub-ons alphabet, ribbon, ribbon charms, photo anchor and mini brads: Making Memories

Flower punch: EK Success

Computer font: AL Modern Type

Label maker tape: Dymo

Other: ledger paper

PAGE 44 MAGGIE HOLMES

M

1. Randomly place rub-ons alphabet over large piece of cardstock to create matte
2. Attach photo, placing it off-center, so more of the matte can be seen
3. Embellish with ribbon and a metal monogram

Simply fabulous trims, vintage hip trinkets, ribbon, monograms (metal), pins and rub-ons alphabet: Making Memories

Marker: ZIG

PAGE 45 MAGGIE HOLMES

LUCKY

1. Cut strips out of patterned paper and then cut each edge on a 45° angle
2. Stack all strips together, and cut simultaneously (The edges will line up for perfect mitered corners)
3. Embellish with flowers, felt ribbon and letter stickers

Simply fabulous paper and monogram alphabet (maddi), felt ribbon, crystal brads, blossoms, MM kids stickers (bella) and blossoms (wildflower): Making Memories

Orange cardstock: Bazzill

Flowers: Prima

Marker: ZIG

PAGE 46 KRIS STANGER

EIGHT

1. Cut moulding strips to desired length (This side will be straight, the top and bottom pieces will have an angle on both sides)
2. Paint entire strip white, let dry, and then gently brush peach across top and edges
3. Trim off 1½" of floral paper and glue down to pink vintage hip 9" x 9", exposing behind of page (The entire sheet of this paper behind the floral will support the weight of the frame)
4. Glue down trims and add decorative pin and rub-ons
5. Place photographs and frame
6. Cut tag out of pink vintage cardstock and add ribbon (This will tuck behind framed photo and contain your journaling)

Vintage hip paper (paisley), trinkets, trims and border stickers (gracen), photo corners, moulding strips (baroque), acrylic paint (white and peach), rub-ons alphabet (red) and rub-ons wordage (love): Making Memories

+ VARIATION 1

1. Use same technique as above as frame is cut and painted
2. Place frame directly onto front of card, wrapping ribbon trim around frame before attaching
3. Add accent pin and rub-ons

PAGE 47 JENNIFER JENSEN

MY 2 SONS

1. Cut four lengths of ribbon pieces to desired length (measure enough for each side of photo)
2. Lightly adhere two pieces around photo
3. Secure by placing decorative brads in corner where both pieces of ribbon intersect
4. Repeat process three more times until frame is complete

Vintage hip ribbon, trinkets and trims, deco brads, crystal brads, rub-ons and paper: Making Memories

+ VARIATION 1

1. Repeat previous process, replacing deco brads with buttons in each corner

PAGE 48 MARIA GRACE ABUZMAN

RELAX

1. Cut a Metal Mesh sheet to 6" x 8" and adhere behind photo as a matte
2. Using similar colors, add trim and embellishments to left side of photo, opposite journaling
3. Type journaling onto complimentary colored cardstock
4. Add rub-ons alphabet as highlight for beginning paragraph

Simply fabulous trims and paper (meg), petite signage, washer words, rub-ons alphabet, metal mesh, rub-ons images, mini brads and safety pins: Making Memories

+ VARIATION 1

1. Print out two copies of the same photo in the same size (One photo will serve as the matte)
2. Cut off ½" on all sides of first photo
3. Adhere trim under cut photo, leaving just a little to peek beneath
4. Place modified photo on top of original-sized photo (The photo underneath now acts as a matte)
5. Embellish with blossoms and rub-ons

PAGES 49 - 51 LONI STEVENS

PHOTOGRAPHY. A PASSION OF MINE

1. Matte both sides of photo with brackets
2. Type brackets and print onto chipboard
3. Cut out
4. Apply double-stick tape to brackets
5. Pour glitter over double-sided tape and tap off extra

Simply fabulous trims (meg), crystal brads, silver snap and monograms (metal): Making Memories

Embossing template (circle): Lasting Impressions

Glitter and tape: Art Accentz and Provo Craft

Font used on photo: Trade Gothic

Computer font: Quick Type

Other: foam core

+ VARIATION 1

1. Cut a circle out of chipboard.
2. Cover with double-sided tape
3. Pour glitter over double-sided tape and tap off extra

ALWAYS AND FOREVER

1. Paint chipboard letters and frame around photo

Vintage hip paper (gracen) and findings, gameboard alphabet, acrylic paint, foam stamps, washer words and crystal brads: Making Memories

Cardstock: Chatterbox

Coin envelope: Bazzill

Photo corner die-cut: QuickKutz

Embossing powder: Ranger

Computer font: Quick Type

9 THINGS ABOUT ME

1. Cut an opening out of vellum to fit over photo
2. Apply vellum over photo and patterned paper by machine stitching it down

Vintage hip paper and buttons (paisley) and frames, jigsaw alphabet (poolside number), petals and paper: Making Memories

Photo corner die-cut: QuickKutz

Clip: Provo Craft

Rub-on numbers and tan cardstock: Chatterbox

Embossing powder: Ranger

Computer font: Trade Gothic Condensed, Quick Type and Times New Roman Italics

PAGES 54 - 55 MAGGIE HOLMES

LOVE

1. Arrange title on block of paper and surround it with random chipboard letters
2. Paint title in different color and emboss with polka dots to make it stand out
3. Embellish with ribbon and charm

Jigsaw alphabet (poolside), MM kids trims (ethan) and cardstock (ethan and sam), ledger paper, chipboard letters, acrylic paint, ribbon labels, felt ribbon and mini brads: Making Memories

Red cardstock: Bazzill

Ranger: UTEE

Rubber stamp: Hero Arts

Ink: VersaMark by Tsukineko

Marker: ZIG

NAUGHTY NEWT

1. Create a large photo corner out of ledger paper
2. Use a variety of stickers to create title
3. Embellish page with patterned paper strips, ribbon and defined stickers

Vintage hip paper and letter stickers (paisley), felt ribbon, MM kids fresh stickers, ledger paper, mini brads, defined stickers and cardstock: Making Memories

Red cardstock: Bazzill

Ribbon: All My Memories

Letter stickers: Chatterbox

Marker: ZIG

PAGES 56 -57 ERIN TERRELL

WHEN BOREDOM SETS IN

1. Add blue border to bottom of green polka dot paper
2. Print journaling on yellow cardstock using Incognitype font, trim and add to upper right corner with ribbon just below journaling
3. Add white borders to photo, then place on yellow cardstock
4. Place file folder so it peeks out from under the yellow cardstock
5. Add dates and journaling to file folder and paint chipboard letters
6. Add rub-ons and photos to blue border
7. Once dry, attach chipboard title to page and finish with brads in the upper right corner of the layout

Vintage hip paper (paisley), gameboard alphabet (sadie), acrylic paint and mini brads: Making Memories

Other: paper

+ VARIATION 1

1. Trim card shape out of solid blue paper
2. Trim strip of yellow cardstock and use black ink for edges
3. Add rub-ons along the bottom of the yellow cardstock
4. Spread modge podge to top of chipboard letters, then place them face down on back of polka dot paper and trim to size
5. Lightly sand edges of chipboard letters and place them on the card with a gameboard flower to dot the 'I'
6. Add ribbon in upper left corner
7. Add a metal tag, place rub-ons on tag and hold in place using ribbon

TLAQUEPAQUE, AZ

1. Cut a scrap of red paper and lightly sand it to create journaling block
2. Run block through printer with journaling done in Incognitype font
3. Add rub-ons to bottom of journaling strip
4. Cut a strip of yellow cardstock for title and use black ink for edges
5. Spell out title using rub-ons and adhere strip to layout
6. Place metal ribbon label over left side of title strip and adhere with brads and ribbon scraps
7. Add remaining rub-ons, ink edges of heart and add a scrap of green polka dot paper in the upper right corner

Textured paper, vintage hip paper (paisley), rub-ons alphabet, mini brads and ribbon label: Making Memories

+ VARIATION 1

1. Trim background cardstock
2. Add striped border to bottom and edge with black ink
3. Add green trim over the patterned paper
4. Lightly sand the scrap of red paper
5. Add rub-ons around the edges
6. Add photo flips to upper left corner of sample
7. Add rub-ons to the title/metal sign

PAGES 58 - 59 LYNNE MONTGOMERY

THE USUAL

1. Trim lighter background paper so border of darker background paper is visible
2. Cut a long rectangular opening down left side of lighter background paper
3. Adhere a long rectangular piece of patterned paper to darker background paper (so it can be seen through rectangular cut-out when lighter background is placed on top)
4. Adhere lighter paper to darker paper, leaving the rectangular opening free from adhesive
5. Create title by stamping on a transparency using acrylic paint
6. Let dry and adhere photos
7. Place transparency and attach the left side with hinges and right side with snaps
8. Adhere envelope on top of transparency, insert journaling strips and finish with tied ribbon on left edge of layout

MM kids paper and trims (kate), double dipped paper, hinges, snaps, brads, jump ring, attachment assortment (valentine), foam stamps (jersey), acrylic paint and gameboard alphabet (lexi): Making Memories

Computer font: Courier New

Others: ribbon, envelope and transparency

CARD PARTY

1. Use a foam brush and spread a layer of acrylic paint over foam stamps
2. Stamp directly onto your project

MM kids paper and trims (kate) and foam stamps (philadelphia): Making Memories

PAGE 60 ERIN TERRELL

YOU CAN TAKE MY PICTURE

1. Arrange photos on various layers in Photoshop, size and create black borders around each shot
2. Create a text layer and add title using AL Highlight font
3. Merge all photos together into one document and print
4. Trim red cardstock to 9" x 9" and adhere photo
5. Add striped paper along bottom border of page as well as ribbon tape along the right border
6. Trim a strip of mustard yellow cardstock and print the journaling on it using Incognitype font and brown ink and ink edges with brown ink
7. Add rub-ons and one additional photo that has been changed to black and white, and place it under the clear frame

Sheer frame: Making Memories

Ribbon and flower: Heidi Swapp

Other: paper

+ VARIATION 1

1. Trim red paper to 6½" x 3" and create fold marks at the ½" mark and another three inches in
2. Use MS Word to create text box and fill with words "Happy Birthday"
3. Print in brown ink on the front of the card (the last 3" fold)
4. Add ribbon tape to the bottom fold of the card (the ½" fold)
5. Add a scrap of yellow cardstock to front of card and ink the edges with brown ink, add rub-ons and attach blossom with brad
6. Hold bottom flap closed with brad and tie a ribbon

PAGE 61 SHERELLE CHRISTENSEN

LET IT SNOW

1. For title, combine handwriting with other elements such as rub-ons, computer text or stamping
2. Create small journaling block, using your own handwriting
3. Use colored pencils that coordinate with your layout to highlight words

MM kids paper and trims (sam), rub-ons, foam stamps, acrylic paint and stickers: Making Memories

Other: ric rac, fabric and colored pencils

PAGES 62 - 63 JOANNA BOLICK

HARPER KATE

1. Layer rub-ons
2. Tear paper edges
3. Adhere ric rac behind vintage hip findings

Vintage hip paper (paisley), trims, buttons (gracen) and findings and rub-ons alphabet: Making Memories

Computer font: Gabriel and Carpenter

SANTA COLE

1. Stamp snowflake background
2. Wind ribbon and lace around patterned paper
3. Secure photo by overlapping it between ribbons

---

4. Attach letters to ribbon using brads and safety pins
5. Write text with white pen and place below photo

Brads, safety pins, vintage hip ribbon, foam stamps, cardstock, acrylic paint and patterned paper: Making Memories

Pen: Uniball Signo white

PAGE 64 JENNIFER JENSEN

LESSONS IN LIFE

1. Print photo and quotations onto label paper
2. Adhere fabric alphabet letters directly onto photograph for title
3. Dot 'i' with small button

Simply fabulous trims (maddi), cardstock printed, fabric alphabet and tiny alphas: Making Memories

Other: buttons and lace

Full sheet label: Avery

+ VARIATION 1

1. Choose word for title and cut fabric letters in half
2. Print saying or quote onto background paper
3. Adhere cut letters to top and bottom of printed title

PAGE 65 KRIS STANGER

MY FRIEND PAIGE

1. Layer trims at bottom and trace a light mark for two straight stitches before attaching trims (this makes it easier to maneuver paper through machine)
2. Place photos
3. Tuck in tag
4. Stamp wordage
5. Lightly glue gameboard pieces and stitch straight through
6. Gently sand gameboard pieces to distress

Cardstock, dyeable trims and tags, vintage hip buttons and trims (paisley), gameboard alphabet (sadie) and ribbon: Making Memories

Computer font: Dragonfly

Other: studio walnut canvas paper, stampin up (close to cocoa ink) and alphabet stamp set

+ VARIATION 1

1. Apply rub-ons to buttercup cardstock
2. Cut rectangular opening and glue down from inside
3. Glue letters lightly into place on tag, and sew using a zigzag stitch directly through wordage
4. Tie tag to card

PAGES 68 - 69 MARIA GRACE ABUZMAN

I LOVE YOU

1. After adhering to cardstock, overlay photo with various clear defined stickers
2. Add various trim and lace to the bottom of photo, running the entire length of cardstock
3. Run another ribbon along edge of photo, bordering photo on top and left sides
4. Use alphabet rub-ons for title, going over defined stickers
5. Using a decorative-edged scissor, cut around patterned paper and add journaling, tucking this behind photo

Vintage hip paper, trims (gracen), trims (paisley) and findings, tiny alphas, defined (romance), rub-ons alphabet (evolution upper and lower white), gameboard flowers (kraft), crystal brads (clear) and acrylic paint: Making Memories

Cardstock: Bazzill basic papers

Ribbon: May Arts

JH

1. Run book binding tape along one side of cardstock and use foam shape stamp to create a unique decoration
2. Adhere photo to cardstock using molded photo corners on left side

3. Tuck a blossom embellishment inside a label holder and adhere to cardstock with brads

4. Use tacky glue to place gameboard alphabets on top of label holder's rim, creating title

5. Using a decorative-edged scissor, cut around patterned paper and add journaling, tucking this behind the photo

Vintage hip paper and trims (gracen), gameboard alphabet (sadie), label holders, brads, blossoms (hydrangea), book binding tape (variety 2), acrylic paint and foam stamps (floral dingbats): Making Memories

Cardstock: Bazzill basic papers

PAGE 70 - 71 LYNNE MONTGOMERY

SERIOUSLY SILLY

1. Lightly sand all patterned paper and adhere to right side of layout

2. Mount photos on white cardstock and adhere to layout

3. Attach ribbon over right side of photos

4. Trim calling cards and attach to sanded patterned paper squares with a shaped clip and photo anchor

5. Slip squares behind photo matte for placement

6. Create monogram by lightly sanding top of metal letter and then apply two coats of acrylic paint to letter and frame

7. After paint is dry, use foam brush and lightly paint over surface in different color

8. Tie monogram to frame with ribbon, back with sanded patterned paper and adhere to layout

Simply fabulous paper, trims (meg) and calling cards, ribbon, charmed frame, acrylic paint, photo anchor, mini brads, shaped clip and monograms (metal): Making Memories

Paper: Bazzill

Photo font: CK Heritage

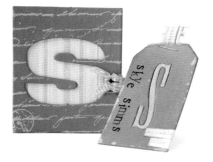

+ VARIATION 1

1. Paint a jigsaw alphabet piece with acrylic paint and when dry, apply a different color to a script rubber stamp and place over piece

2. Tie two pieces of ribbon to the right side

3. Adhere sanded, patterned paper to the back so it shows through the opening

+ VARIATION 2

1. Paint jigsaw alphabet pieces with acrylic paint

2. Cut notches at the top to resemble a tag shape

3. When dry, lightly sand edges

4. Rubber stamp words down one side

5. Wrap words around lower right edge

6. Staple ribbon on top

VICTORY

1. Create computerized border and journaling and cut into strips

2. Ink edges with black ink and adhere to background

3. Create tabs by sticking clear defined words onto vellum metal-rimmed tags

4. Line up tags so most surface is under photo and tape to back of photo

5. Adhere photos to layout, matting the three smaller photos in one strip

6. Ink the edges of the matte strip with black ink

7. Create title by sticking clear defined words to cardstock, trim to size, ink edges lightly with black ink and attach to layout with mini brads and ribbon ends

Vellum tags, defined stickers (clear), mini brads, ink sponge and ribbon: Making Memories

Paper: Bazzill

Computer font: Times New Roman

Other: ribbon

PAGE 72 MARIA GRACE ABUZMAN

PARK PHOTO

1. Attach photo in allotted place on perspectives paper

2. Decorate photo with various rub-ons in upper corner of photo

3. Place an artistic tag on top of fabric swatch

4. Adhere label holders to tag, using at least two different sized holders

5. Create title, using stickers within label holders

6. Cut fabric swatch in half and lay down beneath photo

7. Embellish with trim on top

8. Journal on paper strips, finishing off journaling with rub-ons alphabet

Paper (perspectives), cardstock printed, fabric swatches, fabric tags, vintage hip trims (gracen), leather label holders, tiny alphas, brads, rub-ons alphabet, rub-ons mini and woven corners: Making Memories

Photo corner: Kolo kraft

PAGE 73 LONI STEVENS

A CRAZY GOOD TIME

1. Paint chipboard flowers various colors with craft paint

2. Arrange and adhere flowers down the left side of page

3. Cover the two flowers that are painted a different shade with sheer blossoms

4. Randomly place gem stickers at center of some of the flowers

Chipboard flowers, gem stickers and petals: Making Memories

Paint: Americana (dusty rose and coral rose)

Computer font: Rockwell and Quick Type

PAGE 74 KRIS STANGER

JOY

1. Cut a 9" x 9" piece of dusty rose cardstock and a piece of brown cardstock just slightly smaller

2. Cut two squares of dusty rose (any size) for top right and lower left corners

3. Place photograph in center, print out quote on clear label paper and attach at bottom

4. Paint jigsaw alphabet letters with peach paint, let dry and gently rub in chocolate chip ink with finger

5. Add ribbon across bottom, attach brad and add lettering

Double dipped cardstock, ribbon card, vintage hip alphabet stickers, jigsaw alphabets, alphabet charms, deco brads and acrylic paint: Making Memories

Ink: Stampin' Up (chocolate chip)

PAGE 75 JENNIFER JENSEN

BELOVED ADDISON

1. Layer ribbon onto page and lightly adhere

2. Place row of tags slightly under last piece of ribbon and lightly adhere

3. With sewing machine, straight stitch tags onto page

Cardstock paper, photo anchors and rub-ons: Making Memories

Flower tag: basic grey

Computer font: CAC Champagne

Other: flower and ribbon

PAGES 76 - 77 MARIA GRACE ABUZMAN

SUMMER FUN

1. Trim white cardstock with decorative-edged scissors and use this as photo matte
2. Attach trim to label holder and place along left edge of photo
3. Create title using various alphabet rub-ons in different colors and embellish title with rub-ons images
4. Journal on transparency and adhere to photo

Simply fabulous trims (maddi), label holder, rub-ons images, rub-ons alphabet and rub-ons mini:
Making Memories

SUN FUN

1. Apply paint to foam shape and stamp design on cardstock, creating a unique background
2. Apply secondary paint color in small dots using the tip of a paintbrush on top of original stamped image
3. Once all paint is dry, adhere ribbon to cardstock alongside the photo
4. Decorate chipboard tags with secondary paint color
5. Mix up darker paint with lighter paint to create different shades of color and use these different shades to paint chipboard
6. Once paint is dry, apply modge podge to crystallize embellishments
7. Adhere chipboard to cardstock using painted decorative brads
8. Finish design with alphabet stickers and rub-ons
9. Journal on transparency and adhere to photo

Simply fabulous velvet alphas, gameboard tags, deco brads and rub-ons mini: Making Memories
Other: ribbon and paper

PAGES 78 - 79 LORI BERGMANN

NANA AND KAITLYN

1. Cut diagonally across metal frame with scissors to make four corner pieces, being careful to make a smooth edge
2. Set aside two of the corners and paint the other two with Meadow green paint and let dry
3. Add another layer of Manilla paint and while still damp, rub off the raised areas with a baby wipe to reveal some of the green base coat

Papers, vintage hip buttons (gracen) and metal frame (dot), blossoms (hydrangea cream), page pebbles (friendship), vellum circle tag, cardstock (celery), naked line trims, magnetic stamp alphabet (rummage), acrylic paint and metal glue: Making Memories
Fluid chalk ink: Clearsnap

WHO, WHAT, WHEN, WHERE?

1. Cut diagonally across metal frame with scissors to make four corner pieces, being careful to make a smooth edge
2. Set aside two of the corners and paint the other two with Meadow green paint and let dry
3. Add another layer of Manilla paint and while still damp, rub off the raised areas with a baby wipe to reveal some of the green base coat

Vintage hip paper, trims and buttons (gracen) and frame and acrylic paint: Making Memories
Fluid chalk ink: Clearsnap
Fineliner pen: Staedtler

+ VARIATION 1

1. Apply Meadow green paint on words and borders
2. Very lightly daub a layer of Manilla on top
3. Daub border on with green paint, then rub while still damp

PAGES 80 - 81 MELLETTE BEREZOSKI

COUSIN, FRIEND

1. Apply glue stick to surface of gameboard heart
2. Adhere dictionary page, centering desired word on gameboard heart
3. Turn heart over to back and trim excess paper with x-acto knife
4. Apply diamond glaze over dictionary paper and let dry completely for a glass-like effect

MM kids paper (kate), cardstock printed, gameboard shapes, rub-ons images, ribbon charms, word fetti stickers and defined stickers: Making Memories
Textured cardstock: Bazzill Basics
Printed twill: 7 Gypsies
Dimensional adhesive: Diamond Glaze and JudiKins
Computer font: 2PS Tuxedo
Other: dictionary pages

ANY OCCASION GIFT TAG SET

1. Apply glue stick to surface of gameboard hearts
2. Adhere varying paper coverings to hearts
3. Attach to tag shaped card, using dimensional adhesive

MM kids paper and ribbon (kate), vintage hip trims (paisley), gameboard shapes, rub-ons wordage, word fetti stickers, brads (flower), mini brads, cardstock printed, ledger paper, deco brads and defined stickers:
Making Memories
Dimensional adhesive: Diamond Glaze and JudiKins
Photo sticker: Pebbles Inc.

PAGE 82 SHERELLE CHRISTENSEN

BABY

1. Paint chipboard letters and shapes to coordinate
2. Paint over metal embellishments then wipe off excess

Simply fabulous paper (brooke), vintage hip trims (paisley), gameboard alphabet (sadie), gameboard shapes, ribbon label and charmed words: Making Memories
Other: vintage lace and button

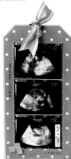

+ VARIATION 1

1. Add paint to charm for instant coordination

PAGE 83 JOANNA BOLICK

TEENY TINY TOOTSIES

1. Adhere patterned papers to cardstock
2. Using photo-editing software, print photo and adhere
3. Handwrite journaling on small strips of cardstock and adhere
4. Embellish three ribbons and adhere
5. Print out and trim small photo
6. Place small photo in center of buckle and adhere

Simply fabulous paper, ribbon charms and trims (brooke), vintage hip trims, safety pin and ribbon charms:
Making Memories

+ VARIATION 1

1. Cluster flower brads around center of buckle
2. Adhere with glue dots

PAGES 84- 85 JENNIFER JENSEN

CLASSIC CHLOE

1. Tie basic knot on end of ribbon, then slide other end through center of photo anchor until the knot is reached
2. Place small amount of glue under knot, adhering to anchor
3. Adhere photo anchor onto edge of photograph
4. With extra ribbon, wrap around edge of base paper, adhere to back and trim

Cardstock paper, photo anchors and rub-ons: Making Memories

Flower tag: basic grey

Computer font: CAC Champagne

Other: flower and ribbon

CURLY Q

1. Layer ribbon onto page and lightly adhere
2. Place row of tags slightly under last piece of ribbon and lightly adhere
3. With sewing machine, straight stitch tags onto page

Simply fabulous trims (brooke), MM kids trims (ethan), gameboard tags, blossoms (hydrangea) and rub-ons alphabet: Making Memories

Computer font: Typo Upright

Other: heart and flower bead and large ribbon

+ VARIATION 1

1. Layer ribbon onto page and lightly adhere
2. Place piece of ribbon through hole on tag and wrap around ribbon border
3. Knot ribbon to hold in place

PAGES 88 - 89 SHERELLE CHRISTENSEN

SWEET BABY

1. Create a minibook to contain all your treasured memories and stories
2. Adhere to layout
3. Create little pockets by sewing two pieces of chenille to page
4. Tuck journaling and memorabilia inside

Simply fabulous paper and trims (meg), chipboard letters, chipboard flowers, ribbons and metal phrase: Making Memories

Purple swiss dot ribbon: May Arts

Other: chenille and lace

MIRACLE

1. Fold piece of cardstock lengthwise
2. Add special journaling inside and adhere to page

Simply fabulous paper and trims (meg), defined stickers (clear), blossoms (wildflower), brads and safety pins: Making Memories

PAGES 90 - 91 LONI STEVENS

BOYS WILL BE BOYS

1. In Microsoft Word create a text box, then type words inside of it
2. Select fill option, then choose color for background fill
3. Highlight text and change font color to white
4. Print and cut into strips

Metal mesh, large woven label, screw snaps, chipboard shapes and acrylic paint: Making Memories

PLAY

1. Determine size of pocket and cut vellum to same size
2. Punch an opening in vellum with square punch where photo will be exposed
3. Type and print journaling onto transparency sheet
4. Cut transparency to fit perfectly over vellum and secure over each other with temporary adhesive at corners
5. Use just enough adhesive to hold it in place as pocket is machine stitched to page
6. Cut photo matte to fit inside of pocket
7. Leave extra space at top to pull photos in and out

Cardstock, silver snaps, gameboard tags, gameboard alphabet (sadie) and acrylic paint: Making Memories

Photo corner die-cut: QuicKutz

Corner rounder: EK Success

Computer font: Andale mono and You Can Make Your Own Font

Transparency: Hammermill

Other: vellum

PAGE 92 MELLETTE BEREZOSKI

SOCCER DAD

1. Use metal charmed frame as template and trace on back side of patterned and textured paper
2. Cut at markings
3. Print journaling on transparency paper and trim to fit behind frames, then adhere to back
4. Attach frames to page using foam tape for added dimension

Paper, gameboard alphabet, MM kids trims, fresh stickers and paper (ethan), charmed, eyelet shapes and petite signage: Making Memories

Textured paper: Fiber Mark

Transparency paper: 3M

Computer font: Times New Roman by Microsoft Word

PAGE 93 LYNNE MONTGOMERY

H3

1. Piece together background papers and add metal mesh to right hand section and a strip of ribbon to left hand section
2. Adhere large main photo so right edge is flush with section where metal mesh and middle meet
3. Create four large tags using shipping tag as stencil and paint edges
4. String ribbon charm alphabet letters onto ribbon and attach vertically where photo and metal mesh meet

5. Tie a piece of ribbon to two tags and attach vertically at each end of the ribbon charm alphabet letters, securing with a mini brad

6. Create computerized journaling blocks, edge with paint and attach to tags

7. Trim metal mesh to resemble tag shape and wrap it around left side of layout, securing with staple

8. Add piece of ribbon for tie and repeat steps for additional tag

9. Embellish metal mesh tags with painted jigsaw alphabet pieces and photo

MM kids paper and trims (ethan), ribbon charm alphabet, mini brads, metal mesh, jigsaw alphabet and acrylic paint: Making Memories

Computer font: Times New Roman

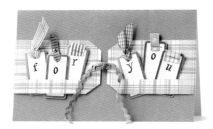

+ **VARIATION 1**

1. Trace shipping tag onto patterned paper and cut out

2. Cut horizontal slit across bottom portion of each tag

3. Wrap ends of tags around card and tie tags together with ric rac in center

4. Rubber stamp and tie ribbons to metal rimmed tags and insert through slits of patterned paper tags

PAGE 94 LYNNE MONTGOMERY

SNOWBALL

1. Cut two long envelopes one third of the way down from top

2. Edge envelopes, photos, shipping tags and background paper with acrylic paint

3. Paint charmed quote and eyelet letters

4. Adhere envelopes to left side of layout

5. Add journaling and trim to shipping tags and place inside envelopes

6. Adhere photos, charmed quote and ric rac trim down right side of layout

7. Use round closure circles and string from an additional envelope and attach vertically to right side of layout with mini brads

8. Add ribbons, paper tags and eyelet letters to envelopes and vertical string

Cardstock, cardstock tags, eyelet letter (classic), jump rings, charmed quote, acrylic paint, ribbon, naked line shipping tags and trims and brads: Making Memories

Other: envelopes, ribbon and trims

Computer font: Courier New, CK Thick Brush and CK Stylish Black

PAGE 95 LORI BERGMANN

ASHLEY

1. Use foam brush to coat diamond stamps with shopping bag acrylic paint

2. Randomly daub on manilla paint and stamp on paper to create background

3. Lightly brush manilla acrylic paint along edges of layout and shopping bag paint on ledger paper

4. Stamp name, bullet designs and journaling words on ledger paper with brown and pink inks

Papers (pink cosmopolitan), ledger and vintage hip (gracen), foam stamps (diamond), chipboard flowers, acrylic paint and magnetic stamps (rummage, express it and ornaments alphabets): Making Memories

Fluid chalk ink: Clearsnap

PAGE 96 LONI STEVENS

BEAUTY

1. Fold patterned paper in half like a card, to create door

2. Fold same size piece of patterned paper for inside

3. Attach the two pieces together for cover and inside of door, leaving bottom right corner open for vellum

4. Add photo and attach door to layout

5. With circle punch, punch hole through all three layers (photo and two sheets of cardstock)

6. Attach index tab to small piece of vellum and slide through two sheets of paper for cover and inside of door

7. Secure vellum with adhesive, but don't seal the two pieces of paper yet

8. Add circle tag rub-ons over vellum window

9. Print desired text within the rub-ons on a transparency and secure over vellum, inside the two sheets

10. Seal the two pieces of cardstock closed and add journaling and photos inside

11. Add photo anchor towards top to keep flap down

Cardstock printed, foam stamps (patterns), rub-ons mini, metal frame, rub-ons images, rub-ons alphabet, photo anchor, brads, petite signage and staple: Making Memories

Computer font: Haettenschweiler, Lacuna Regular, Quick Type and You Can Make Your Own Font

Index tab: Avery

Embossing powder: Ranger

Other: vellum and transparency

+ **VARIATION 1**

1. Cut a rectangular piece of white cardstock for door

2. Open card and trace that same piece of cardstock onto one side of folded card

3. X-acto knife around three sides of pencil marks to create flap for door

4. Glue rectangular piece of white cardstock down over cutout and cut inside of flap with x-acto knife to create a frame on door for vellum window

5. Cut fitted piece of vellum for window

6. Stamp polka dot image on vellum, then line the inside of frame with it

7. Close card and adhere the outside rim together, making the door the only component that opens

PAGE 97 KIMBERLY BEE

BABY AIDEN

1. On solid background, adhere vintage hip paisley paper on left-hand side leaving one end open, forming a pocket

2. Line right-hand side of background with vertically placed photos and paisley accent square

3. Add smaller solid square and button on top

4. Journal on plain scalloped paper and attach with one side open, like a folder

5. Add ribbon vertically on left-hand side, with paisley paper accent in middle of bow

Cardstock, vintage hip paper, buttons and trims (paisley): Making Memories

PAGE 98 MAGGIE HOLMES

NATHAN

1. Open photo in Photoshop and use type tool to type journaling directly onto photograph
2. Change color of text to match layout and vary size and font of journaling
3. Print picture and journaling onto photo paper
4. Embellish page with patterned paper, ribbons and paper clips

Vintage hip paper and trims (gracen), ledger paper, photo anchor and mini brads: Making Memories

Other: paper clips

Computer font: ScoutlightDB and Fabianestem

PAGE 99 MARIA GRACE ABUZMAN

GLOW

1. Trim patterned paper ¼" on each side.
2. Ink edges and place on top of cardstock
3. Create a vertical title, place it directly on photo and embellish with crystals
4. Create journaling using alphabet rub-ons and definition stickers
5. Highlight individual words within the definition by placing a coordinating piece of cardstock directly below that word

Vintage hip paper (gracen), rub-ons alphabet, gameboard alphabet (sadie), gem stickers and defined stickers (clear): Making Memories

Ink: ColorBox Black

PAGES 102 - 103 MELLETTE BEREZOSKI

FAMILY

1. Crop photos to 2" x 7"
2. Print journaling on a 7" x 2" piece of cardstock
3. Arrange photos and journaling block across page
4. Add trim, fabric flower, and button to top of journaling block
5. Apply rub-on images to last photo

Vintage Hip paper, buttons and trims (paisley), petals, rub-ons images, and embossed stickers: Making Memories

Computer font: Arial by Microsoft Word

FOURTH BIRTHDAY

1. Cut four photos to 2" x 7"
2. Print journaling on a 7" x 2" piece of cardstock, folding metal rim tag over top
3. Arrange photos and journaling block across page
4. Add button over metal rim tag

Cardstock printed, MM kids trims and paper (ethan) and button (sam), defined stickers, metal rim tag, label holder, jelly label, jigsaw alphabet (numbers poolside) and mini brads: Making Memories

Computer font: Times New Roman by Microsoft Word

FALL

1. Cut an 8" x 7" photo into four 2" x 7" pieces and attach to page
2. Print journaling on cardstock, punch hole at top and tie ribbons and attach to page
3. Add painted leaf charm and leather corner

Cardstock printed, ledger paper, jigsaw alphabet (poolside), paint, eyelet charm, cosmo ribbon and snaps: Making Memories

Floral paper: Chatterbox

Computer font: Messenger by Autumn Leaves

PAGES 104 - 105 JENNIFER JENSEN

SAFETY AND SECURITY

1. Cut four strips of various ivory papers, coordinating to match base 12" x 12" page
2. Cut strips of paper measuring 2" x 12", 3" x 12", 4" x 12" and 5" x 12", then fold each strip in half, keeping it twelve inches in length
3. Lightly adhere paper strips to all four edges of 12" x 12" base
4. Using accent color of thread, straight stitch with machine around inside edge of each strip to create page binding

MM kids trims (bella), paper, charmed and magnetic stamps: Making Memories

OH HAPPY DAY

1. Cut strips of various red papers, coordinating to match base 12" x 12" page
2. Complete using instructions above

MM kids trims (kate), cardstock smooth, charmed and magnetic stamps: Making Memories

A DADDY AND A DAUGHTER

1. Cut strips of various white papers, coordinating to match base 12" x 12" page
2. Complete using instructions above

MM kids trims (ethan), cardstock smooth, charmed and magnetic stamps: Making Memories

PAGES 106 ERIN TERRELL

GYM SHOES

1. Create photo and journaling elements using Adobe Photoshop

2. Print and place on background of embossed red cardstock
3. Add gameboard shapes and place smaller photos on top

Cardstock printed, gameboard shapes, rub-ons images and ribbon: Making Memories

A LOOK LIKE THIS

1. Create photo and journaling elements using Adobe Photoshop
2. Print and place on background of embossed red cardstock
3. Add gameboard shapes and place smaller photos on top
4. Add ribbons to gameboard shapes and adhere with glue dots
5. Add decorative rub-ons
6. Add gameboard shaped heart in upper left corner and adhere with mini glue dots
7. Trim strip of red cardstock and emboss with small circles, then add to right-side border

Vintage hip paper and trims (paisley) and rub-ons images: Making Memories

PAGES 107 LYNNE MONTGOMERY

HAPPY 2005

1. Start with a 9" x 9" square of patterned paper and adhere one solid 6" x 6" square in upper left corner and another in lower right corner
2. Make the matte/tag in right corner by cutting square of solid cardstock and rounding corners
3. Cut smaller square and round corners and fold smaller square over top of larger one and adhere on the backside, then ink edges black
4. Position everything on the background
5. Tack photo down using adhesive in center (leaving edges loose) and tack matte/tag down in right corner
6. Trim clear defined word strips to right size and adhere to layout, slipping the edges under photo
7. Once in place, secure photo and matte/tag with additional adhesive
8. Tie ribbon and label holder around layout
9. Embellish pockets, adhere to layout and slip journaling strips inside

Cardstock printed, gameboard alphabet (sadie), ribbon, cardstock tags, vintage hip trims (gracen), jump ring, defined stickers (clear), rub-ons, ink sponge and eyelet charmed tags: Making Memories

TRADITION 2005

1. Start with a 9" x 9" square of patterned paper and adhere one solid 6" x 6" square in upper left corner and another in lower right corner
2. Make the matte/tag in right corner by cutting square of solid cardstock and rounding corners
3. Cut smaller square and round corners and fold smaller square over top of larger one and adhere on the backside, then ink edges black
4. Position everything on the background
5. Tack photo down using adhesive in center (leaving edges loose) and tack matte/tag down in right corner
6. Trim clear defined word strips to right size and adhere to layout, slipping the edges under photo
7. Once in place, secure photo and matte/tag with additional adhesive
8. Tie ribbon and label holder around layout
9. Embellish pockets, adhere to layout and slip journaling strips inside

Cardstock printed, gameboard alphabet (sadie), ribbon, cardstock tags, simply fabulous trims (maddi), jump ring, defined stickers (clear), rub-ons, ink sponge and eyelet charmed tags: Making Memories

Paper: Bazill

Computer font: Wendy Medium

Other: gingham ribbon and rubber stamps

PAGES 108 - 109 SHERELLE CHRISTENSEN

THAT CRAZY, SILLY, GOOFY, WACKY HAT

1. Divide background into four sections
2. Incorporate one large photo and one small photo
3. Use remaining two sections for title and journaling
4. Change up colors, add buttons and layer ric rac and ribbon

Woven ribbon, label holders, ribbon card, safety pin and rub-ons alphabet: Making Memories

Other: ric rac

JUST US GIRLS

1. Divide background into four sections
2. Incorporate one large photo and one small photo
3. Use remaining two sections for title and journaling
4. Change up colors, add buttons and layer ric rac and ribbon

Woven ribbon, label holders, ribbon and safety pin: Making Memories

Other: ric rac

PAGES 110 LONI STEVENS

2 DEVOTED

1. Punch ribbon slits on rectangular chipboard tags
2. Paint tags green and sand edges
3. Stamp polka dots on green tags with versamark and emboss with brown embossing powder
4. Adhere tags next to one another on page between photo and journaling and place blossoms between two tags
5. String ribbon through slits and secure left side with snap
6. Cut a larger #2 out of chipboard
7. Paint and machine stitch down left side of number
8. Double stitch around entire page

Scalloped paper, MM kids trims (ethan), chipboard tags, blossoms, petals (sheer), crystal brads and silver snaps: Making Memories

Paint: Delta Technical Coatings (leaf green) and Americana, Deco Art (colonial green)

Embossing powder: Adirondack (espresso)

Polka dot stamp: B-Line Designs

Photo corner die-cut: QuicKutz

Graphic icon rub-ons (white dots): KI Memories

Ribbon slot punch: McGill

Computer font: Perma Petit and Quick Type

Other: chipboard

2 PERSONALITIES

1. Punch ribbon slits on rectangular chipboard tags
2. Paint tags green and sand edges
3. Stamp polka dots on green tags with versamark and emboss with brown embossing powder
4. Adhere tags next to one another on page between photo and journaling and place blossoms between two tags
5. String ribbon through slits and secure left side with snap
6. Cut a larger #2 out of chipboard
7. Paint and machine stitch down left side of number
8. Double stitch around entire page

Scalloped paper, MM kids trims (bella), chipboard tags, blossoms, petals (sheer), crystal brads, silver snaps, calling card stickers and acrylic paint: Making Memories

Paint: Delta Technical Coatings (fuchsia)

Embossing powder: Adirondack, Ranger (moss)

Polka dot stamp: B-Line Designs

Ribbon slot punch: McGill

Computer font: Times New Roman Italics by Microsoft Word: Perma Petit and Quick Type

Other: chipboard

PAGES 111 MARIA GRACE ABUZMAN

ALOHA STYLE

1. Cut patterned cardstock to 8" x 8" and white cardstock to 3" x 8"
2. Use decorative-edged scissors to trim white cardstock
3. Lay down various embellishments around the journaling piece, making sure they strongly compliment photo
4. Use alphabet rub-ons to create title

Cardstock printed, blossoms (hydrangea), mini brads, rub-ons alphabet and rub-ons images: Making Memories

THE HAPPY GRAD

1. Cut patterned cardstock to 8" x 8" and white cardstock to 3" x 8"
2. Use decorative-edged scissors to trim white cardstock
3. Lay down various embellishments around the journaling piece, making sure they strongly compliment photo
4. Use alphabet rub-ons to create title

Cardstock printed, blossoms (hydrangea), mini brads, rub-ons alphabet and rub-ons mini: Making Memories

PAGES 112 - 113 JOANNA BOLICK

LET THE JOURNEY BEGIN

1. Cut tin frame in half to create two photo corners
2. Layer cardstock and patterned papers
3. Print journaling on cardstock and adhere
4. Adhere photos
5. Attach photo corners
6. Add decorative detail to bottom photo corner

Vintage hip paper (paisley) and frames and metal signage: Making Memories

SIMPLY IRRESISTIBLE

1. Use your own handwriting rather than printed text for softer appearance

Cardstock prinnted, vintage hip paper (gracen), metal signage and MM kids trims (ethan): Making Memories

OUTDOOR ADVENTURE

1. Use patterned papers rather than solids and substitute metal signage for tag

MM kids paper (ethan) and trims (sam), vintage hip frame, well worn tag and acrylic paint: Making Memories

Computer font: Abuse light

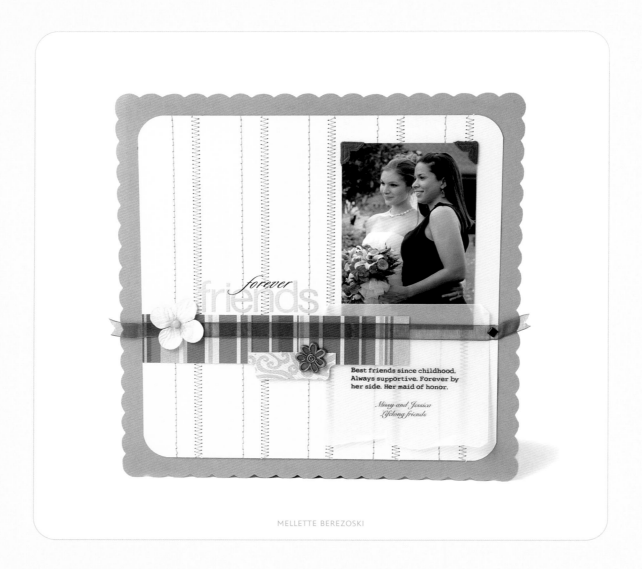

forever
friends

Best friends since childhood.
Always supportive. Forever by
her side. Her maid of honor.

Missy and Jessica
Lifelong friends

MELLETTE BEREZOSKI

MELLETTE BEREZOSKI

MAGGIE HOLMES

MAGGIE HOLMES

SHERELLE CHRISTENSEN

Joe is coaching Dayton's soccer team this year. He is so good with young kids. He is very encouraging and enthusiastic. He teaches them drills and basic skills, does cheers with them, and makes sure they are all laughing and having a fun time.   2005

MELLETTE BEREZOSKI

How do you enjoy
your day?

By gracing it with a
smile, enjoying the
sun, and laughing
out loud.

smiles

2 o o 5

MARIA GRACE ABUZMAN

MELLETTE BEREZOSKI

LONI STEVENS

MARIA GRACE ABUZMAN

MAGGIE HOLMES

KIMBERLY BEE

MELLETTE BEREZOSKI CROSBY, TEXAS

Mellette is a stay-at-home mom and reality-TV junkie who admits that she's a messy scrapbooker but likes to clean up in-between projects. When not working on an assignment, you'll most likely find her on her back porch browsing through mail order catalogs, flipping through her old book collection or admiring her flower garden.

MAGGIE HOLMES SOUTH JORDAN, UTAH

Even though she's the mother of three boys, Maggie is all girl. A self-confessed fashionista, she's currently working on expanding her growing collection of purses and bags. Always cheerful, smiling and organized, the one thing she'd have if she were stranded on a desert island would be TiVO.

JENNIFER JENSEN HURRICANE, UTAH

A self-described Coke-only drinker (no diet!), Jennifer is terrified of snakes, mice and heights. But that doesn't stop her from doing the things she loves — trailer camping, cooking and baking, eating eggs for breakfast, exercising and talking on the phone for hours.

LYNNE MONTGOMERY GILBERT, ARIZONA

Lynne's most recent accomplishment is that she ran in her first 10 mile race. And she had plenty of time to train since she hasn't watched television in the last five years. She is an avid collector of hair magazines, loves homemade blackberry pie and can hardly buy anything without a coupon.

KRIS STANGER ST. GEORGE, UTAH

To Kris, there's nothing finer than a good pedicure and manicure. Since she's the mother of four, including a newborn, a little pampering is just what she deserves. Other loves include Bath and Body Concentrated Room Spray, planting flowers in the spring, Oprah and the color green in every shade.

LONI STEVENS PLEASANT GROVE, UTAH

You'll rarely find Loni without a Diet Dr. Pepper in her hand and good tunes playing in the background. Born on the day Mount St. Helen's erupted in 1980, she's a devoted family gal whose childhood dream was to be a makeup artist/hair stylist to the stars.

ERIN TERRELL SAN ANTONIO, TEXAS

Originally from South Carolina, Erin confesses that her least favorite household chore is cleaning up her scrapbook room. She'd much rather be enjoying the spring weather, reading InStyle magazine, grilling outside, traveling or taking landscape photography.

JULIE TURNER GILBERT, ARIZONA

The Château de l'Isle-Marie in France and the Hotel Del Coronado in California. Just a couple of the interesting places in Julie Turner's "collection" of interesting places to stay. When not traveling to exotic locales, she manages to stay busy home schooling her three children, working on projects and remodeling her house.

CREATIVE DIRECTOR OF PUBLICATIONS

GAIL PIERCE-WATNE MURRAY, UTAH

Although relatively new to the scrapbooking industry, Gail Pierce-Watne is no amateur in the world of design. Her longtime passion began when she designed the bulletin boards for her first grade class. When Gail is not working, designing or running in marathons (she's run in 15 to date), she is with her family. She believes her greatest talent in life, next to her near-perfect impersonation of Shania Twain, is raising an outstanding family.

CONTRIBUTING ARTISTS

MARIA GRACE ABUZMAN UNION CITY, CALIFORNIA   **KIMBERLY BEE** TOLLESON, ARIZONA

LORI BERMANN STILWELL, KANSAS   **JOY BOHAN** BEDFORD, INDIANA

JOANNA BOLICK FLETCHER, NORTH CAROLINA   **SHERELLE CHRISTENSEN** SHELLEY, IDAHO

be inspired.™